FOR THE LOVE
OF MONEY AND
THE BIBLE

BY
ALAN DALE DICKINSON

This book is a actual story, a research project and not a work of fiction. References and incidents are also real as to the memory and recollection of said author. Without limiting the rights under copyright reserved above, no part of this publication may be reproduced, stored in or introduced into a retrieval system, or transmitted, in any form, or by any means [electronic, mechanical, photocopying, recording, or otherwise], without the prior written permission of both the copyright owner and the publisher of this book. The scanning, uploading, and distribution of this book via the Internet and via any other means without the permission of the publisher/owner is illegal and punishable by law. Please purchase only authorized electronic editions, and do not participate in or encourage electric piracy of copyrighted materials. Your support of the legal rights of the author is greatly appreciated.

DICKINSON, ALAN DALE

"FOR THE LOVE OF MONEY'

c/o: Dickinson and Sons
        Alan D. Dickinson
        Chairman and Chief Executive
        Officer (Retired) AND
        Corporate Vice President
        Bank of America
        (Retired)
        P.O. box 180
        La Habra, CA 90633-0180

DEDICATION

This book: "FOR THE LOVE OF MONEY" (Volume I) is dedicated to my beloved grandson "Scott Alan" and my precious granddaughter "Morgan Marie" the best grandkids in the whole wide world. I hope that the rest of you grandparents out there will understand [smile].And my brilliant and very dependable eldest son David Alan and his wonderful, lovely and smart wife, Desiree'. With my strong and dedicated second son Mark Alan and his multi-talented new bride, Ramona.

And, to my Highly intelligent sister, Susan Lee Dickinson Smith. Also, to my wonderful and saintly mother, Vivian Lee Martin Dickinson. My beloved mother and best friend in the whole wide world, went home to heaven to be with our Lord and Savior on August 2, 1999 at 11:00 p.m. I was there, thank God, to say goodbye to her, and at the same moment, God was welcoming her in to Heaven.

ACKNOWLEDGEMENTS

This book "For The Love of Money," [Volume I] might never have come to fruition had it not been for the encouragement and assistance of a few very kind hearted people. At the top of my list, special thanks are due to my best friend in the whole wide world, Curt Rouanzoin, and also my good friend (and adopted brother) Carl Mascarella. They have more love and Christian compassion than anybody I have ever met in my entire life. To Rhonda, for her wonderful organization and computer skills. Without her I would have been at a huge loss. She is one of the best Christian's I have ever met in my life.

In the final analysis, this book is the product of the Love God has shown to me all of these many years here on 'old' planet earth.

FORWORD

Have you noticed lately that everyone seems to be writing a book about money? Even if they do not know very much about it, did not have any expertise, and/or do not have a background in business or the Banking industry. I have presented herewith an book about money based upon the Bible (the Scriptures) and historical facts. I have however, included a little insight from my twenty-five (25) years in the Banking and Business arena. I hope that will be alright, ha, ha. I hold an Business Administration Degree from the School of Business Administration
and Economics [with concentrations in the business subjects of: a) accounting, b) economics, c) finance, d) management and, c) real estate, at California State University - Fullerton. In addition, I hold an Life Time teaching Credential in Business and Banking from the State of California, Department of Education, for any Community College in California. Also, I had a securities license (Stock Broker) for the sale of stocks, bonds and mutual funds as well as an   State   of California Insurance License to sell Life Insurance, Retirement Plans and annuities.

I did not, unfortunately, I am sorry to say, receive my Masters of Business Administration M.B.A. (in Management) from California State Fullerton. Someday, however, I hope to complete my subject M.B.A.

I was born in downtown Los Angeles during an earthquake, on the side of the Harbor Freeway (just kidding) at the famous California Hospital. I think it's famous, anyway. That makes me a native Californian. People from California seem to move out of state. People from out-of-state seem to move to California. This does not make a lot of sense to me. I am not   sure   what   a "native" is, however, some people are very impressed when they find out that I am one. I have traveled a lot, however, I have never found any place I like better than right here. Maybe that is what a native is. Someone who likes it right here in sunny Southern California. I love L.A.; I really do.

We really never have earthquakes in Southern California. That is just a modern day myth. They only happen in Northern California (and Mammoth Mountain). Los Angeles is the City   of Angeles, and they do not allow anything "more than a gentle rolling" in their town.

FOR THE LOVE
OF MONEY
AND THE BIBLE

VOLUME 1

BY
ALAN DALE DICKINSON

TABLE OF CONTENTS

CHAPTER I

CHAPTER I
MONEY: THE ROOT OF ALL EVIL?

First of all, right here in the first chapter please allow me to correct an age old myth: "Money" ($) is not the root of all evil. More simply put, it is the "LOVE" of money, that is the root of all evil (according to the Bible).

"Keep your lives free from the <u>love</u> of money, and be content with what you have." Hebrew 13:5

Many times we (you and I) take several precious blessing's for granted. We murmur instead, if "I only had a newer/nicer car (or S.U.V.); a higher paying job; some new clothes; was better looking; was taller or shorter; was smarter; and/or had more money ($); etc., etc., etc., <u>Then</u> I would be happy and <u>content</u>." But, would we (I) really? The Bible teaches very clearly, that we would not be any happier than we are right now in our present circumstances. Yes, I personally feel that things would be much easier and more palatable, however, not really any happier.

<u>Evil Money</u>

Matt. 6:24 "No one can serve two masters. Either you will hate one and <u>love</u> the other, or you will be devoted to the one and despise the other. You cannot serve both God and money
(mammon).

I Cor. 16:2 "On the first day of every week, each one of you <u>should</u> set aside a sum of money in keeping with your income, saving it up, so that when I come no collections will have   to   be made." (Some say extra missionary offering over and above your regular giving tithe, etc.)

I Tim. 6:10 "For the <u>love</u> of money is a root of all kinds of evil. Some people, eager for money, have wondered from the faith and pierced themselves with money grief's."

<u>Bible</u>

I heard a pastor say once that there are more verses about money in the Bible than any other topic, except God and His love. I did not count them, so if this is incorrect, please do not blame me, ha, ha.

<u>Love of Money</u>

If anyone teaches false doctrines and does not agree to the sound instruction of our Lord Jesus Christ and to Godly teaching, he is conceited <u>and</u> understands nothing. He has an unhealthy interest in <u>controversies</u> and <u>quarrels</u> about words that result in envy, strife, malicious talk, evil suspicions and constant friction between men of corrupt mind, who have been robbed of the truth and who think that Godliness is a means to <u>financial</u> gain.

But Godliness <u>with contentment</u> is great gain. For we brought <u>nothing</u> into the world, and we can take <u>nothing</u> out of it. But if we have food and clothing, we will be content with that.

People who want to get rich fall into temptation and a trap and into many foolish and harmful <u>desires</u> that plunge men and women into ruin and destruction. "<u>FOR THE LOVE OF MONEY IS A ROOT OF ALL KINDS OF EVIL</u>." Some people, eager for money, have wandered from the faith and pierced themselves with <u>many</u> grief's.

"Command those who are rich in this <u>present</u> world not to be arrogant nor to put their hope in wealth, which is so uncertain, but to put their hope in God, who richly provides us   with everything for our enjoyment. Command them to do good, to be rich in good <u>deeds</u>, and to be generous and willing to share. In this way they will lay up <u>Treasure</u> for themselves as a firm foundation for the <u>coming</u> age, so that they may take hold of the life that is turfy life."

Many war's (oppressive invasions and police actions, etc.) are started so that the attacking country can get more land, precious metal (gold) and/or more <u>money</u>. Wealthy people never seem to feel that they have enough money, I am not sure why that is (human nature)? Some people will rob, steal, and murder for money (and valuables). Killing is one of the oldest sins in human history and the Bible, (mo' money, mo' money, and mo' money, as an old saying goes.)

<u>Being content (with little money):</u>

Make a list of all your favorite belongings and possessions. Be sure to include things like your house, car's, your different clothes, etc. Read I Timothy 6:6-10. What is really important in life is Godliness (being God's person) and having enough to eat and to wear. People who think they have to have more things and more money to be happy are usually unhappy and discontented no matter <u>how</u> much they have.

<u>The Rich Young Man:</u>

As Jesus started on his way, a man ran up to him and fell on his knees before him. "Good teacher," he asked, "what must I do to <u>inherit</u> eternal life?" "Why do you call me good?" Jesus answered. "No one is good—except God alone. You know the commandments: 'Do not murder, do not commit adultery, do not seal, do not give false testimony, do not <u>defraud,</u> honor your father and mother.' "Teacher," he declared, "all these I have <u>kept</u> since I was a boy." Jesus

looked at him <u>and loved him</u>. "One thing you lack," he said. "<u>Go. sell everything you have</u> <u>and</u> give to the poor, and you will have treasure in heaven. <u>Then</u> come, follow me." At this the

man's <u>face</u> fell. He went away sad, because he had great <u>wealth</u>. Jesus looked around and said to his disciples, "How hard it is for the <u>rich to enter</u> the kingdom of God!" The disciples were amazed at his words. But Jesus said again, "Children, how hard it is to enter the kingdom of God! It is easier for a <u>camel to</u> go through the eye of a needle then for a rich man to <u>enter the</u> kingdom of God. The disciples were even more amazed, and said to each other, "Who then can be <u>saved</u>?" Jesus looked at them and said, "With man this is <u>impossible,</u> but not with God; all <u>things</u> are possible with God." Peter said to him, "We have left <u>everything</u> to follow you!" I tell you the truth," Jesus replied, "no one who has left home or brothers or sisters or mother or father or children or fields for me and the gospel <u>will fail to receive a hundred times as</u> much in this present age (homes, brothers, sisters, mothers, children and fields - and with them, persecutions) and in the age to come, eternal life. But many who are first will be last, and the last first."

Mark Chapter 10 (v. 17-31) seems to indicate (at least to myself) that having a lot of money may, just may, be a drawback to getting into Heaven, (see v.22-24). The rich young Ruler chose his earthy money ($) over eternal treasure in Heaven. At least on that given day. Let's hope that later on he changed his mind and accepted Christ. God gives us all second (third, fourth, etc.) chances. Thank God for that, right? While Jesus clearly points out here in   Mark,   that   "it   is easier for a camel to go through the eye of a needle than for a rich man" (one who covets and has the love of money as the root of his/her heart and soul) "to enter the Kingdom of God."

Then, however, in V. 27 He states "all things are possible with God." Even a camel going through the needles eye. Once again, it was not so much the fact that the young man was rich as much as it appears to me, his 'love of money.' If you happen to be wealthy and are reading this said book, please take note of this section of the Bible and its important message.

Denarii (Money) and Judas
(Mark 14:1-11)

Now the Passover and Unleavened Bread was two days off; and the chief priests and the scribes were seeking how to seize Him by stealth, and kill Him; for they were saying, "Not during the festival, lest there be a riot of the people." And while He was in Bethany at the home of Simon the leper, and reclining at the table, there came a woman with an alabaster vial of very costly perfume of pure nard; and she broke the vial and poured it over His head.   But   some   were indignantly remarking to one another, "Why had this perfume been wasted? "For this perfume might have been sold for over three hundred (300) denarii and the money given to the poor." And they were scolding her. But Jesus said, "Let her alone; why do you bother her? She has done a good deed to Me. "for the poor you always have with you, and whenever you wish, you can do them good; but you do not always have Me. "She has done what   she   could;   she   has anointed My body beforehand for the burial. "And truly I say to you, whatever the gospel is preached in the whole world, that also which this woman has done shall be spoken of in memory of her." And Judas Iscariot. who was one of the twelve, went off to the chief priests, in order to betray Him to them, and they were glad when they heard this, and promised to give him money. And he began seeking how to betray Him at an opportune time.

Judas had the love of money ($) in his heart as you can plainly see from the above verses.

CHAPTER II

CHAPTER II
The History of Money

[Money: a medium of exchange (then and now)]

Gold. Frankincense, and Myrrh:

Scripture References:

"Now when Jesus was born in Bethlehem in the days of Herod the King, behold there come wise men from the east...and when they had opened their treasure, they presented unto him gifts: gold, frankincense, and myrrh." Matt. 2:1-11

Gold for royalty. This coin is an authentic replica of an actual coin from Parthia, the land of the Wise Men. It was just such a coin as this that must have been part of their gift! On one   side their king (Verdanes) is shown between two stars. On the other, a first century telescope is shown, pointing at the heavens. Although glass was not used, it served to shut out all stars except the one they wished to watch. Real barreled gold has been used in the reproduction. King Verdanes ruled at the time of Christ. Frankincense for worship. A tribute to the divinity of Jesus, incense was made from fragrant drops of gum, which came once a year from certain trees in Arabia. The incense in this package came from the original source. Myrrh for healing. Still used as medicine in all lands, myrrh was one of the most potent healing herbs used in Bible times. It symbolized Jesus' concern for healing.

Coins of The Bible

1. Herod the Great	37 B.C. - 4 B.C.	
2. Stater of Antioch	27 B.C. - 14 AD.	
3. Shekel of Tyre	1 B.C. - 14 A.D.	
4. Herod Antipas	4 B.C. - 40 A.D.	
5. Widow's Mite (Capanius)	6 A.D. - 9 A.D.	
6. Tribute Penny (Tiberius)	14 A.D. - 37 A.D.	
7. Lepton (PonTius Pilate)	26 A.D. - 36 A.D.	
8. Shekel	66 A.D. - 70 A.D.	
9. Half Shekel	66 A.D. - 70 A.D.	
10. Dilepton (Simon Nasi)	66 A.D. - 70 A.D.	
11. JudeaCapta (Vespasian)	-70 A.D.	

12.	Shekel	- 133 A.D.	
	(Bar Kochba)		
13. Quarter Shekel		132 A.D.	-
14. Denarius		135A.D.	
		132A.D. - 135 A.D.	

The treasure chest of the 'wise men':
Gold, Frankincense and myrrh.

1. Herod The Great
37 - 4 B.C.

When Antipater, procurator of Judea, was killed, he was succeeded by his second son know as Herod the Great. Herod leaned toward Greek culture and was a man of violent jealousies and passions. It was during his reign that Jesus was born. Mary and Joseph fled to Egypt to save the life of Jesus for Herod the Great had ordered the death of all male children up to two years of age. The lepton shows a Macedonian helmet on the obverse. A tripod used on the reverse to demonstrate Herod's pagan spirit was possibly copied from Greek coins. The bronze coin was made from melted down implements owing to a scarcity of other metals. Matthew 2:16-18... "And sent forth and slew all the children that were in Bethlehem and in all the coasts thereof, from two years of age and under, according to the time which he had diligently inquired of the wise men."

2. Stater of Antioch
27 B.C.-14 A.D.

This replica of the Tetra drachma of Antioch in Syria may also possibly be the type of silver coin given to Judas for the betrayal of Christ. On the obverse is a portrait of Emperor Augustus. The reverse depicts a female figure representing the Tyche of Antioch with the river Orontes at her feet. Matthew 26:15... "And said unto them what will ye give me, and I will deliver him unto you? And they covenanted with him for thirty pieces of silver."

3. Shekel of Tyre
1 B.C. -1 A.D.

The thirty pieces of silver paid to Judas by the Pharisees for the betraying of Christ are thought to be this four drachma replica of the Phoenician City of Tyre. The shekel, acceptable as Temple dues, was referred to as "Tyrian money." the obverse shows a laureate head of Melkarth, a Phoenician god in the form of the Greek god Hercules. An eagle stands on a ship's bow with a palm branch in the back ground. The legend in Greek reads, "Tyre sacred and inviolable sanctuary." The club is a symbol of Melkarth.

4. Herod Antipas
4B.C.-40A.D.

This ruler known as the tetrarch, was the son of Herod the Great, and his original heir. He married for a second time, Herodias, who had been the wife of his brother. He built Tiberius in honor of his patron, the notorious Emperor Tiberius, where he issued his coins. This replica has a palm branch, the title, "Herod Tetrarch" and a border of dots on the obverse. The reverse has a wreath with "Tiberius" in Greek, in the center. As a result of his relations with Herodias, he put St. John the Baptist to death. Matthew 6:14-27... "For Herod himself had sent forth and laid hold upon John and bound him in prison. For Herodias' sake, his brother Philip's wife, for he had married her...and when the daughter of the said Herodias came in and danced and pleased Herod...the king said unto the damsel ask me whatsoever thou wilt. And she came in...and asked saying I will that thou give me by and by, on a platter, the head of John the Baptist."

5. Widow's Mite
Capanius 6-9 A.D.

The smallest of Greek bronze coins. The word "mite" was used in the Bible and was obviously referred to as the smallest coin known and used by the Jews. St. Luke 21:1... "And he looked up and saw the rich men casting their gifts into the treasury. And he saw a certain poor widow casting in thither two mites. And he said, of a truth I say unto you that this poor widow hast cast in more than they all. For all these; Have of their abundance cast in unto the offerings of God; but she of her penury hast cast in all of the living she had."

6. Tribute Penny
Tiberius 14-47 A.D.

This coin, called "penny" in the 1611 - King James Version of the Bible, should be called "tribute denarius." In ancient times, while the Roman legions occupied Britain, the denarius was the standard coin. Tiberius was the Roman Emperor who ruled during Jesus' lifetime. St. Mark 12:14-16... "Is it lawful to give tribute to Caesar or not? Shall we give, or shall we not give? But he, knowing their hypocrisy said unto them. Why tempt ye me? Bing me a penny, that I may see it. And they brought it. And he said unto them, Whose is this image and superscription? and they said unto Him, Caesar's. And Jesus answering said unto them, Render to Caesar the things that are Caesar's and to God the things that are God's."

7. Lepton
Pontius Pilate 26-36 A.D.

Pontius Pilate, known to all Christians for his delivery of Jesus to the Crucifixion, was governor of the Holy Land. He came from the household of Tiberius and was probably a freedman. The coin shows a simpulum (ladle) said to be a sacred vessel presented to the Temple by Tiberius. The obverse has three ears of grain bound together. The Legend reads, "Money of Julia Caesar" (wife of Tiberius). Reference to this controversial governor is: John 18:28-19:42... "Pilate then went out unto them, and said, what accusation bring ye against this man?..."

8. Shekel
66-70 A.D.

Authorities believe that these thick shekels were struck during the First Revolt of the Jews, 66-70 A.D., and were issued in each of five years during this period, dated from year one to five. The coin shows the golden cup, a chalice from the vessels of the Temple, which held   the Manna. On the reverse is a branch of three pomegranates in transition from flower to fruit, considered to be the most famous of ancient Judean coin symbols. The inscription in ancient Samaritan reads "Jerusalem Kenosha" (Jerusalem the Holy).

9. Half Shekel
66-70 A.D.

It is believed that these thick half-shekels were also struck during the First Revolt of the Jews, 66-70 A.D., and were issued in each of five years during this period, dated from year one to five. This replica of the half-shekel is from the third year of the Roman Jewish War.   The inscription in ancient Hebrew script "Shazi Hasekel" (Half Shekel) and the date "SH' (nat) "G" (immel) year three, appear above the chalice. On the reverse also are the three pomegranates in symbolic transition from flower to fruit.

10. Dilepton
Simon Nasi 66-70 A.D.

Silver and copper coins with inscriptions in Hebrew were struck by Elizar. They were dated years 2, 3, and 4 of the First Revolt. The amphora on the obverse, as a Temple motif, served as a inspiration symbol during the Bar Kochba Revolt. It bears the legend, "Deliverance of Israel." The vine leaf on the reverse represents one of seven kinds of fruit frequently mentioned in the Bible. This replica is a well known copper piece of Simon Nasi. (Nasi means chief or prince.)

11. Judea Capta
Vespasian 70 A.D.

This replica is one of many coins which were struck in Palestine by the Romans, reminding the Jews of their defeat in the First Revolt. The obverse shows the Emperor Vespasian with the legend, "Imperator Caesar Vespasianus Augustus." The reverse reads, "Judea   Capta,"   and   shows a date palm tree (symbol of Judea) with the Emperor on the left and a weeping Jewess seated with head bowed on the right. The words to the Prophet Isaiah foretold this condition to the Jewish people: Isaiah 3:25, 26... "Thy men shall fall by the sword, and thy mighty in the war...And her gates shall lament and mourn. And she, being desolate, shall   sit   upon   the ground."

12. Shekel
Bar Kochba 133 A.D.

This silver shekel replica is from the Second Revolt. The obverse shows the Ark of Covenant and two scrolls of the law. The inscription, "Shimon," presumably refers to the first name of Bar Kochba, the heroic leader of the Revolt against Emperor Hadrian. Simon called himself the Messiah, son of a star (Bar Kochba). The reverse shows esrog (citron) and lulav (bundles of twigs) associated with the Feast of the Tabernacles.

13. Quarter Shekel
132-135 A.D.

Coins of the Second Jewish Revolt were struck over Roman denarii and drachmas of Antioch. Sometimes the original designs showed through. This replica of a quarter shekel has a grape cluster and the legend, "Simon," on the obverse. The reverse has two trumpets and the legend, "Deliverance of Jerusalem." Grapes and the vine, and juice of the grape enter recorded human history early in the Bible. The husbandry of the vineyard is noted after the flood: Gen. 9-20... "And Noah, the husbandman began, and planed a vineyard."

14. Denarius
132-135 A.D.

Coins of the Second Jewish Revolt were also struck over Roman denaii and drachmas of Antioch. They generally had biblical symbols such as musical instruments, palm branches and grapes. The legend on this replica reads, "Simon," and has a lyre with three stings. The lyre, as a Temple instrument, served to remind Jerusalem's defenders of the reason they were fighting. On the reverse is a palm branch in a wreath with the inscription, "Of the   Deliverance   of Jerusalem."

In the time of the New Testament, a day's pay was a single coin (called a Denarius in Matthew 20:2). This was just enough money to buy food for one (1) day and to rent a 'small' room for one (1) night (about $200.00 U.S. today). The coin was made of silver and was usually stamped with a picture of the Roman Emperor. It looked somewhat like our U.S. dime (.10 cent coin) today.

More Ancient Coins

1. The Widows Mite (Regular) 100 B.C. - 60 A.D.
[Not the Capanius Widows mite]

It is said that Jesus told his disciples about the Widow's Mite, "This woman has given more than all of the rich men. They have plenty of money and gave only a small amount to the temple treasury. This woman had only two small coins and she gave all she had." Mark 12:41-42.

The Widow's Mite is the term used in the King James version of the Bible in referring to the smallest coin in use between 100 B.C. and 60 A.D. Also known as a lepton, these coins were typically struck in
bronze.

2. Giordian III (Roman Silver Coin) 238 A.D. - 244 A.D.

These well-preserved Silver relics tell the story of the Roman Empire. Dated from 238 to   244 A.D., the coin features a portrait of Giordian III, the ruler under whom it was minted.

This coin is at least 1,700 years old Condition: very fine.

3. Constantine the Great 307 A.D. - 337 A.D.

Constantine I, the Great, Emperor of Rome (307 A.D. - 337 A.D.) is best remembered for his conversion of the Roman Empire from paganism to Christianity. Constantine coins were struck in bronze, silver and gold throughout the Roman world during his reign. This 1500-year old ancient treasure had been hand-cast of bronze and remains a lasting tribute to the first Christian Ruler of Rome.

4. Madonna and Child 1540 A.D. -1600 A.D.

This ancient silver coin is famous for its beautiful Madonna and Child image. Hand-struck from 1540 through 1600 in what is now Hungary, it became one of Europe's most revered coins
during Europe's late Renaissance period.

The front depicts the Virgin Mary and Baby Jesus; the back has the date the coin was struck. This coin is authenticated to be at least 400 years old.

Shot Definition of Money

1. Something generally (universally) accepted as a medium of exchange. A measured of value
   or a means of payment; a) Officially coined or stamped metal currency, and b) paper money.
2. A form or denomination of coin or paper money.

12

3. Wealth reckoned in terms of money. Persons, or companies, possessing or controlling great sums of money.

Money = Life or Death

Money is the life 'blood' of the people, the world and its economy. It's
like black gold machine 'oil' to help keep people and society running.   It's
like 'water' that everyone on this old planet earth has to have to survive.
Like food that we can only go 'so long' (so many days) without. It is
very easy to see, if you just look around the world you and I live in (even in the U.S.A.) that without water, food and a little bit of money people are dying. A lot of people unfortunately.

Money

Money is the medium in which prices are expressed, debts discharged, goods and services paid for, and bank reserves held. When used in the sense of the money supply, the term is synonymous with circulating medium and may be regarded as comprising demand deposits and common money or currency (q.v.); i.e., paper money issued by the government, bank notes and coins. The term is used still more broadly to embrace money which does not enter into   hand-to-hand circulation. This applies to the standard money, often gold, which may be held as a basic monetary reserve without at any time entering into general circulation. In the United States it includes gold certificates which constitute the legal reserves of the federal reserve banks. The term may even be extended to include abstract units which have been employed at different times for stating certain prices, the best known example being the guinea which is still used in England for stating certain types of monetary payments. The expression "near-money"   was coined to identify certain types of liquid assets, such as time deposits and short-term government obligations, which are regarded as possessing some of the important characteristics of money and as having significant effects on the working of the monetary system.

The difficulty of arriving at a single clear-cut definition of money has led to identifying money in terms of the functions it performs. The British economist Ralph G Hawtrey stated   that:
"Money is one of those concepts which, like a teaspoon or an umbrella, but unlike an earthquake or a buttercup, are definable primarily by the use or purpose which they serve." Alternatively, it may be said that money is anything, regardless of its physical or legal characteristics, which customarily and principally performs certain specified functions.

The functions of money (upon which definition depends) are closely interrelated, but it is nevertheless useful to differentiate among them. The most familiar is that of medium of exchange, whereby goods and services are paid for and debts and other contracts discharged. Money is <u>also</u> the unit of account, in which records are kept, costs computed, and   values compared. It is a means of stating the prices of goods and services and expressing debts, salary and wage agreements, rents, insurance obligations, and innumerable other contracts. The <u>third</u>

major function of money is to serve as a reserve of ready purchasing power. Money is the only completely liquid asset. Ownership of a cash balance in the form of currency or demand
deposits makes it possible to act quickly in matters calling for the payment of money. The convenience and other benefits conferred by the possession of ready cash are entirely different from the more or less pathological considerations that motivate the miser.

Certain functions of money which were of major importance at one time declined, while other functions became more important, and entirely new functions arose. The use of money   as   a
store of value was important in earlier societies but became of relatively little consequence in more advanced economies. People now prefer to store values in savings deposits, insurance
policies or securities where the unit-of-account function of money (particularly as a standard of deferred payments) is of primary concern. With the rise of commercial banking   and   central
banking came a corresponding increase in the importance of the use of money as reserves of the banking system.

Money is unique among economic goods; it is usually regarded not as wealth (though gold or other commodity money should be included as part of wealth) but as a device for exchanging and measuring wealth. An increase in the quantity of money in a country does not necessarily constitute an increase in the country's wealth. More money would result in higher prices or greater liquidity but would not necessarily, except possibly through some roundabout process, mean greater wealth. Money is neither, a production good nor a consumption good. It is
sometimes given the rather abstract title of "numeraire," something used for counting or relating other things. As such there is no satisfactory means of stating the value of money (its price or what it exchanges for) other than by means of index numbers (q.v.) of prices. Changes in the value of money are shown as the reciprocal of percentage deviations of the index from some established base. A rise of 100% in the index number of prices would signify that the value of money—i.e., its purchasing power—had fallen by one-half.

<u>Origin and Development of Money</u>—Scores, perhaps hundreds, of different object's have

served as money at one time or another, including such things as gunpowder and the jawbones of pigs. Perhaps the heaviest money ever used was the stone money of the island of Yap in the South Pacific, and the lightest, the feather money of the New Hebrides. For centuries,   salt
money circulated among the natives of Ethiopia without being supplanted by the gold or silver coins of the traders with whom the Ethiopians came in contact. At one time it was thought that particular types of money came into existence as a result of the most generally bartered
economic good gradually coming to serve as a common medium of exchange. Such an explanation is hard to reconcile with the adoption of a great many of the monetary types known to history. The ox of Homeric <u>Greece</u> (pekus, from which comes the word pecuniary), the
elephant of <u>Ceylon,</u> or the skull money used in Borneo during the 19th century can scarcely have served widely as a medium of exchange. On the other hand, it is easy to suppose that oxen or elephants may have been used as a basis for comparing the wealth of persons or tribes, and from that they have become the standard for measuring other values as well. Human   skulls
enjoyed unique prestige in the social system of Borneo; it became customary to relate pigs or palm nuts to, this highly regarded unit when comparing their values for purposes of actual exchange. In this way, skulls served as the standard and pigs and palm nuts as the medium of

exchange, just as in western societies gold has served as the standard and coins and paper money as the medium of exchange.

Money is to be thought of as having originated out of Religious and social custom rather than directly out of barter, commodities which later came to be important as a standard of value or medium of exchange seem first to have been important as ransom, bride price, ceremonial
offering, or means of ostentation. The application to economic ends generally developed out of the earlier discharge of religious, legal and ritualistic uses. Early money was often some useful substance. In the evolution of the money material there seems to have been a tendency to move from the more useful substance to the less useful and more ornamental. The popularity of gold and silver, two of the most ornamental of metals, attests to the close relation between money and ornamentation. So also does the frequent use of coins as ornaments and the issuance of coins with holes in them to facilitate stinging. Terms associated with monetary units were once generally related to bases of measurement. Drachma meant handful (originally a handful of iron nails); pound, livra, lira and ruble were terms of actual metallic weight.

In contrast with terms such as pecuniary, drachma and pound, which reflect the commodity origins of money, are the words note and bill which relate to debt. The step from terms denoting physical assets to terms indicating debt is of great significance in the history of monetary
development. It reflects the transition from predominantly commodity money to predominantly debt money. At first, debt money retained a link with the past in the form of   legal   and   other connections with a commodity base such as gold or silver; thus the bank note was originally a promise to pay some sort of asset (i.e., commodity) money. In many modern counties,
however, debt money stands alone without any pretense to commodity backing or to convertibility into any form of asset money. Debt money has assumed a variety of forms, of which demand deposits (so-called cheque-book money) are now the most common.

Resort to the use of debt money removed the basis of the automatic regulation of the money supply by means of market changes affecting a commodity used as money. As long as   the monetary structure was directly tied to gold or silver the volume of money was limited by the physical character of the money substance. Changes in the amount of money in circulation'
were subject to influences from the side of the money material. Although it would be possible to devise a system of debt money which would operate automatically, the effect of the spread of debt money was to lessen the influence of automatic forces and to increase the importance of monetary management and control throughout the world. Because the character of the money itself does not establish effective limits to its issue, the prevention of abuse in the instance of debt money depends upon the exercise of due restraint by the issuing authority. The satisfactory functioning of noncommodity money is dependent on strength   and   responsibility   of   the government and reasonable stability of economic conditions. Such notable instances of monetary breakdown as occurred in Germany in the middle 1920s and in China, Greece and Hungary in the middle 1940s resulted when these requirements were not fulfilled.

Commodity standards embodied a technique of monetary regulation and control. Abandonment of commodity standards and subordination of automatic influences, even where the link with some metallic base remained, contributed to the devising of substitute procedures for governing monetary behavior. These included an expansion in the number and powers of central banks and, most notable of all, the establishment of the International Monetary fund (q.v.) at the end of World War II. If the functioning of these alternative techniques left considerable   to   be desired, the same could also be said of the methods employed earlier.

Monetary Standards—The type of money which serves as the basis for the monetary system of a country and to which other kinds of money are, customarily related, through convertibiling or otherwise, is known as standard money. The effect adopting a particular monetary standard is to make that the basis for measuring value in the same sense that the adoption of the fact or the pound establishes it as the basis of measuring distance or weight. It is to be noted, however, that monetary standard have never provided a unit of measurement comparable with these others
from the standpoint of uniformity and constancy. Monetary standards are of two main types, commodity standards and noncommodity or paper standards. The most widely known commodity standard is gold. The general principles of the gold standard apply to any commodity standard, whether monometallic or not. The essence of the gold standard is maintenance of equality between the value of the domestic currency unit and a stipulated amount of gold. The various provisions for establishing and maintaining the gold standard are to be regarded as means to this end. The international gold standard exists when counties
maintain convertibility between currency and gold and allow the free export and import of gold. With these provisions in effect the domestic currency unit will be equal in value to a given
weight of gold in world markets.

Various types of gold standard have existed at one time or another, differing primarily with respect to the provisions; governing convertibility between currency and gold. The gold coin standard was common until World War I and in some countries until the depression of the
1930s. Under this standard, currency is convertible into gold at the initiative of anyone and for quantities as small as the smallest gold coin available. Under the gold bullion standard, currency and gold are convertible only in large amounts. Convertibility may be further restricted, as by providing that currency will be redeemed only at the initiative of specified groups such as foreign central banks. The gold exchange standard exists where currency is convertible not into gold coin or bullion but into drafts payable in the currency of some country which is on the gold standard. Because this provision will presumably result in equality
between a unit of domestic currency and a given weight of gold, the gold exchange standard is to be regarded as a true form of the gold standard. As a result of the events of the 1930s, government officials in various counties were given unusual powers in connection with the administration of the gold standard. At one time discretionary provisions of this character would have been considered incompatible with a true gold standard. Certain of the discretionary
features were subsequently removed but it remained customary to speak of the modified gold standard in contrast with the traditional gold standard such as formerly existed.

Bimetallism exists when two metals are standard money, each at a fixed price in terms of the domestic currency unit (and therefore, of course, at a fixed ratio in terms of one another).

Bimetallism using gold and silver was widely adopted in the 19th century but its success was far from uniform, partly because different counties attempted to maintain legal ratios which were incompatible with one another. Proposed commodity standards include symmetallism and composite commodity reserve money. Under symmetallism the monetary standard would consist of two or more metals exchangeable at a fixed price in terms of the domestic currency unit when combined in legally fixed proportions. Composite commodity reserve money would differ from synetallism in that the standard unit would comprise not only metals but an assorted group of staple commodities. The aim of the various compound standards is to improve on the gold standard by extending the general principles of monometallism to a broader commodity base. Under a paper standard, currency is not convertible on fixed terms into any specific

commodity or combination of commodities. The paper standard is said to be controlled if transactions involving foreign exchange, and therefore exchange rates in terms of foreign

currencies, are strictly regulated. Degrees of control may vary greatly; sometimes multiple exchange rates are maintained, with different quotations for different types of transaction. A free paper standard differs from the controlled in that transactions involving foreign exchange are relatively unrestricted and exchange rates are allowed to fluctuate. The authorities may undertake, however, to exercise a steadying influence on exchange   rates   as   through   the operations of an exchange stabilization fund.

Circulating Medium—Money as a medium of exchange consist of currency and demand deposits at commercial banks against which cheques (checks) are drawn. The use of bank deposits for effecting current payments largely superseded the use of bank notes and became especially far advanced in Anglo-Saxon counties. In the United States the issue of circulating notes by commercial banks was narrowly restricted after 1866 and prohibited after 1936; only the federal reserve banks now have privilege of note issue. A similar monopoly was given to the Bank of England much earlier. Throughout the world the volume of circulating medium has expanded at a more rapid rate than population or physical volume of business. In 1900 currency and demand deposits in the United States amounted to $52 per capita;   50   years   later   it   was more than 14 times as great. The total, particularly of deposits, tended to decline In depressions. It expanded greatly during wars, with currency growing at a faster rate than deposits.   The aggregate of circulating medium is governed by forces largely outside the control of individuals. The proportions which are held in the form of deposits and currency, respectively, and the particular denominations of currency held, however, are almost wholly determined by the actions of individuals. Increases or decreases in the amount of currency' outstanding or of any particular denomination are largely automatic. The commercial banks, the central bank and the treasury are at any given moment merely the agents through which the   preference   of individuals is expressed.

Meaning of the Value of Money—It is customary to express the value of money in terms of what it will buy. Because money is used to purchase ,an endless variety of things it is necessary to resort to some suitable index of prices as a measure of changes in purchasing power.

Different indexes may be chosen as representative of the purchasing power in different uses or for different groups of people. A rise in the index signifies that a given sum of money will

command fewer things than before, and a fall in the index signifies that it will command more. If the index were to rise from 100 to 200 it would mean that the same amount would buy only half as much; conversely, a decline from 100 to 50 would signify that it would buy twice as much as before. Thus it is said that 'the value of money varies inversely with the price index. Neither the value of money nor the level of prices is to be regarded as changing because of a

17

change in the other. Causality between changes in the value of money and movements of the price index is not involved; they are simply alternative ways of expressing the same idea.

Value of money is most <u>commonly</u> used in the sense just described, that of purchasing power over goods and services. It is necessary, however, to distinguish certain other meanings. The expression may refer to the value of money in terms of some standard money substance. Thus the mint parity that exists under the gold standard is the official value of the currency in terms of the standard commodity, gold. The reference in the <u>U.S. constitution</u> to congress's power to regulate the value of money uses value of money in this sense. Again, value of money may

relate to the price of the monetary unit of one country in terms of the unit of another country. This is what is meant by saying that the pound is worth so many dollars and cents. The interest rate is sometimes referred to as the price of money but this usage is open to the objection that what is priced is not the money itself but its use for a period of time (usually a year). This price is more nearly analogous therefore to ordinary rent, which is the price charged for the use of real property for a period of time such as a year. To criticize the propriety of identifying the

interest rate with the "price" of money is not to deny, however, that interest may be an important factor in the operation of the monetary system.

<u>Source of the Value of Money</u>—Because money came into existence as a result of certain valuable commodities assuming money functions, it was natural enough that value in the commodity use should have been looked upon as the source of value in the money use. The value of commodity money was explained in terms of the value of the commodity used as money; the value of money which, had ceased to be convertible into gold or some other commodity was explained in terms of the prospect of future redemption in some valuable commodity. As long as ,commodity money was predominantly used, this conception of, the source   of   the   value remained common. After the collapse of the international gold standard in the decade of the 1930s, however, much of the world continued year after year to employ money which had no commodity value, was convertible into no money commodity, and had no prospect of future convertibility. Yet in many counties the money continued to maintain its value as successfully as when it had been attached to some commodity base.

When a person accepts a piece of money he does not stop to consider whether it is convertible into gold or has gold reserves behind it; nor does he take account of the fact that the government has declared it to be legal tender. If he were to analyze his motives he would at once realize that he is willing to accept money in exchange for things of value because he has no doubt that he will be able to pass the money on to others in the same way. Thus the value   of   money   is   a <u>reelection</u> of the value of the goods and' services which the users of money find that they can get for it when they choose to pass it on to others. It.is not directly dependent on the money
substance or on government authority.

The commodity feature may conceivably have a bearing on the source of the value of money through affecting its acceptability. This consideration is likely to be important, as has been noted, in the origin of money. Similarly, the action of government in making money legal tender may influence its general acceptance. Once money has become established, however, the absence of these features seems to have little effect on the acceptability of money and therefore

18

on its value. Instead, the principal reason for basing money on some valuable commodity is then that this provision is believed to afford a necessary safeguard against over-issue. Either the commodity aspect or governmental authority is to be regarded as part of the, possible technique of determining the quantity of money, not as a precondition of money's having value.

Causes of Change in the Value of Money—Monetary theorists have long been occupied with the question of what causes the value of money to change. The problem to be explained is why changes take place in the general level of prices. If we think of a collection of economic goods which have been selected as representative of what people spend their money for, the question is why it takes sometimes more and sometimes fewer dollars to buy this aggregate of economic
goods. Changes in the value of money are most commonly explained, especially in the United States, in terms of the transactions form of the quantity theory of money. The formula used in discussing the quantity theory is derived from the self-evident fact that what is sold is equal in value to what is given in payment. Thus the quantity of goods (including securities) and services traded (T) multiplied by their average price (P) is equal to the quantity of money (M) multiplied by the number of times the ,money is used (V) during the period. This is the so-called equation of exchange the total value of what is bought (PT) is equal to the total value money payments made (MV); i.e., $PT=MV$ or $P=MV/T$. There are statistical difficulties in actually applying the equation of exchange. Conceptually, however, it is a simple statement of identity   and   it   is   not   to   be
confused with the quantity theory of money. This theory results only when certain assumptions are introduced with respect to the factors in the equation of exchange. The most important such assumption is that P is passive; i.e., is determined by and not determinant of the quantities M, V and T. The theory then amounts to saying that the value of money changes inversely with and as a result of changes in the quantity of money and its rate of use, and directly with changes in the
volume of trade. Formerly there was a tendency to assume that V and T were relatively stable and therefore that the value of money could be regarded as varying inversely with the quantity of
money alone. Considerable importance is now attached to changes in V and T, especially the former. The emphasis on M is regarded as being justified only for major inflations and then only approximately.

Another form of the quantity theory of money (usually known as the cash-balance form) which has been particularly popular is Great Britain replaces the quantities V and T with k and R when R represents real income and k the proportion of R which the public desires to hold command over in the form of money. The equation $P = M/or$ amounts to saying that the value of money is measured by the goods and services entering into real income varies inversely with and as a result of changes in the amount of money and directly with the desire of the public to hold resources in the form of money. The quantity k is similar to though not quite the same as the reciprocal of V This form of the quantity theory has the advantage of emphasizing psychological influences through k, but in general has much the same shortcomings as the transactions formulation of the theory. Theories such as the foregoing are designed to account in general terms for significant changes in the purchasing power of money. When it comes to a consideration of more specific factors, it is to be noted that major prices have been associated primarily with war. Serious inflation has seldom occurred in peacetime except as a direct aftermath of war. The financial burdens arising out of war typically result in strong pressures toward expansion of the circulating medium and in a weakening of the power of governments to resist these pressures.

<u>Money and the Level of Business Activity</u>—Partly as a result of the depressed conditions of the 1930s, the main interest of monetary theorists shifted to the relation of the operation of the monetary system to the level of business activity. This representation of monetary theory was signalized by the publication in 1936 of the General Theory of Employment, Interest   and Money, by John Maynard Keynes. Formerly, money had been discussed chiefly in relation to its usefulness in facilitation production, exchange and the division of labor generally and to its effect on changes in the price level. Thereafter much greater attention was devoted to the bearing of money payments on levels of employment and economic output. The focus of attention shifted from money stocks to money flows. The theory of money came to be more closely integrated with general economic theory. The assumption underlying this newer approach was that the level of business activity is determined by total effective demand. Total effective demand is defined as aggregate monetary expenditures for final products. Changes in the level of business activity are then explained in terms of factors governing the total volume of expenditures. Directly related to liquidity preference is the rate of interest, which Keynesians defined as the price demanded for parting with liquidity. The rate of interest was assumed to be determined by two factors - the community's liquidity preference <u>and</u> the amount of money in existence.

The relations of saving to investment occupy a position of great importance in monetary theory directed toward explaining how levels of business activity are determined. The issues, aptly technical and partly terminological, are involved. It is sufficient to say here that the <u>inclinations </u>of the public with respect to current saving and investment greatly affect the volume of money payments which governs the level of business activity. Saving is generally regarded as being primarily determined by, rather than a determinant of, the prevailing level of income. Changes in investment are looked upon as ordinarily the principal   immediate   factor   contributing   to variations in total effective demand. The great strategic importance of investment rests partly on the autonomous influences which may originate with it and partly on the extent to which it can be made the object of governmental policies such as those designed to bring about changes in interest rates, the money supply and public works.

Total monetary expenditures may also be described as originating with the three classes of spenders-consumers, investors and government. At one time it was customary to concentrate attention on the first two categories only, but in most counties of the world governmental expenditures had assumed such large proportions by the middle of the 20th century as to warrant separate consideration. Changes in the volume of spending by the government are likely to have a decisive effect on total effective demand in time of war and may remain significantly high even in peacetime. Spending by consumers is much the largest element in aggregate demand. One of the principal modifications of earlier Keynesian monetary theory was to attach greater importance to possible changes in the volume of consumption expenditures. Great importance, though perhaps not so great as at first, continues to be ascribed to spending by investors, with changes in inventories being looked upon as the most significant element contributing to shot-run fluctuations in the volume of investment. The level of total effective demand depends on the combined spending by all three groups-consumers, investors and government rather than on changes in spending by anyone of them alone.

The quantity theory of money and the total spending approach constitute the two principal guides to monetary policy. They are to be regarded as supplementing one another rather than as being in conflict. To some extent they can be directed toward the solution of similar problems, but for the most part the quantity theory tends to be applied to policies relating   to   price movements, especially inflation, and the total spending approach to policies relating to fluctuations in business activity.

Monetary Policy—Monetary policy ordinarily refers to measures employed by the central bank of a country to influence the quantity or use of money for the purpose of promoting economic stability. Monetary policy also may be directed toward other ends such as financing   war   or facilitating recovery from a business depression. The concept may embrace other policies which affect monetary relationships; e.g., the issue of fiat money (inconvertible currency) and
regulation of foreign exchange rates. Monetary policy is distinguished from fiscal policy, even though the latter may be directed toward similar ends. Fiscal policy includes taxation, public works expenditures and management of the public debt where these measures are carried out with a view to influencing business activity. With the enlarged scale of treasury operations,
fiscal policy assumed greatly increased importance. In the division of functions between monetary policy and fiscal policy, monetary policy is often looked upon as being the more effective of the two in combating inflation, and fiscal policy in overcoming deflation. "One of the major problems of monetary policy is that of integrating it with fiscal policy. The two are to be regarded not as alternatives but as complementing one another. Complete independence of the central bank and the treasury is impracticable; the activities of the one inevitably involve those of the other so that the problem of relationships between them is one of co-coordinating the activities of each with those of the other.

The principal instruments of monetary policy may be classified into the two categories of general and selective controls. The general instruments of control in the U.S. include the discount rate, open market operations, and changes in reserve requirements. The discount rate was usually looked upon as most important until the decade of the 1920s, and open market

operations as most important after that time. Instruments in this category are general in the sense that they are directed toward influencing the volume and use of money and credit without regard to any particular use or class of user. The selective instruments, on the other hand, are designed to control the use of money and credit in particular areas; e.g., the stock market,

installment sales, real estate and possibly inventories. While any of the instruments of monetary policy is presumed to alter the market compared with what it would be in the complete absence of control, the general instruments are less open to criticism on the grounds of interfering with the freedom of adjustments through the operation of market forces.   At   one   time,   monetary policy was thought of primarily in terms of maintaining a fixed relationship between domestic currency and a given weight of gold or what amounts to, the same thing, an approximately

constant exchange value in terms of other currencies on the gold standard. After World War I, considerable interest was attached to the idea of maintaining stability in the value of money as measured in terms of some standard index number of prices. Later the goal of monetary

stability assumed broader proportion: it came to be thought of in the sense of a high level of business activity (with due allowance for growth).

The great difficulty with monetary policy lies in the fact that the various possible aims such as those just mentioned, each of which is likely to be economically desirable in itself, may come into conflict with one another. The authorities are certain to be confronted with the' necessity of choosing from among various desirable goals. The problem is one of effecting a balance among objectives, even though the price of making progress in one direction is to fall a little shorter in some other direction. Flexibility is - essential since objectives which were appropriate at one
time may cease to be suitable under changed circumstances. The task of monetary policy, including the balancing of different and potentially conflicting objectives, has become more complex but out at the same time the means at the disposal of the monetary and fiscal authorities have become more numerous and, in total, more powerful. This fact gives rise to the problem already noted of effectively integrating monetary policy with fiscal policy. It   also
involves the problem of co-coordinating the, various instruments of monetary control-the general controls with the selective and one general or selective measure with another. A satisfactory solution of the problems of integration and co-ordination would open the way, despite the greater difficulty of the task, to more comprehensive and effective monetary policy than was possible under former conditions.

International Aspects—The international role of money is an extension of the place it occupies and the functions it performs within a country. The ideal is that, through such means   as   the
adjustment of foreign exchange rates and changes in the money supply, appropriate relationships may be established between the price levels of different counties with the expectation that there-upon the demand and supply of foreign exchange will be equalized automatically and the balance of international payments maintained in equilibrium. The criterion of such an ideal equilibrium is the preservation of a high degree of freedom for individuals to exercise their choice in international economic relations without creating monetary disturbances through excessive drain of monetary reserves, flights of capital, or inflationary or deflationary pressure on prices. Because of the quantitative importance of international trade and its responsiveness to price differences, price-level. Adjustment occupy a strategic place in international monetary affairs. It is to be noted, however, that money   and
monetary policy may also exist an important influence on the level of interest rates in different countries, the movement of short-term and long-term capital changes in business activity, and other economic development. Domestic and international policies are closely related.
Experience after World Wars I and II clearly indicated that unless domestic budgets are brought under a reasonable degree of control there could be little hope of solving the problem of the international balance of payments.

There are two principal methods of bringing the price level at one country into adjustment with the levels in other counties. The method of the international gold standard is that prices should be subjected to pressures calculated to bring them in line, while exchange rates are allowed to remain approximately constant. The method of "free" inconvertible paper currencies is to bring about the adjustment by changes in exchange rates, while prior levels are allowed to remain more or less stable. The gold standard method seeks to make price   levels   conform   to established exchange rate relationships; the paper standard method seeks to make exchange rates conform to prevailing price levels. Under the international gold standard, exchange rates were anchored to the mint par of exchange; i.e., the ratio of the pure gold content of one

22

monetary unit to the pure gold content of the other. Exchange rates could fluctuate on either side of the mint par by no more than the cost of transferring gold from the mint of one country (or similar place of redemption) to the mint of the other country. These limits are known as the gold shipping points. Whenever the exchange rate moved to one of the gold points,   gold reserves would move from the country whose price level was as high to the country whose price level was too low. This would tend to, bring about a contraction of circulating medium in the country where prices were high and an expansion of circulating   medium   in   the   'other country. This in turn would presumably bring their price levels into proper adjustment. Supplementary influences, as by way of changes in incomes and interest rates, were expected to facilitate the entire process.

Under a system of free paper currencies, exchange rates are regarded as being anchored to what is technically known as "purchasing power parity." This is a much less definite point then that which the gold standard provided; it represents a relationship which theoretically will equalize the purchasing power of the currencies over goods, and can be calculated   by   comparing changes in price level indexes from some base year. In actual practice, neither method of price level adjustment worked as perfectly as the description might suggest. The drain of gold reserves sometimes had an unsettling effect public psychology and might even aggravate the existing disequilibrium of the balance of international payments by leading to hoarding/or lights of capital. In addition, countries losing or gaining reserves did not always adjust circulating medium in the manner that was expected of them. Likewise, under paper standard conditions, the foreign exchange value of paper currencies sometimes exhibited erratic fluctuations which, far from serving any useful purpose in effecting an orderly adjustment of supply and demand, might have list the opposite tendency.

The International Monetary fund (I.M.F.) was established at the end of World War II as an

alternative to either a gold standard or a paper standard system. The international gold standard was regarded is having contributed to the spread of depression and as likely to interfere with the success of full-employment policies. Free paper standards were associated in the public mind with inflation and with disorder in the foreign exchange markets.   The   fund   undertook   to promote exchange rate stability by facilitating adjustment of <u>minor</u> fluctuations in the demand and supply of foreign exchange and to permit orderly changes in exchange rates when
fundamental disequilibrium in international balances of payments arises. The bulk of foreign exchange transactions are handled through ordinary channels. Operations involving the fund are carried out between the fund on the one side and the treasuries, central banks or   similar
agencies of member counties on the other side. Member counties are allowed to draw on the fund to meet temporary shortages of foreign exchange, each member country having an assigned quota within which it must stay. Payments in and out of the fund because of short run variations in the demand and supply of foreign exchange operate a substantially the same
manner as the various exchange stabilization funds which have been set up at different times on a more local basis.

It was hoped that the International Monetary fund (IMF) would bring about the removal of direct controls over foreign exchange operations, hold exchange rate changes within narrow limits, and permit the early restoration of convertibility among the various national currencies. That these expectations were not realized may be attributed more to the seriousness of balance of payments difficulties in the years after World War II than to any defects apparent in the fund.

MONEY. MEDIEVAL; The Roman monetary system as reorganized by Constantine the Great included reduction of the weight of the gold coin solidus to 1/72 of the Roman libra (pound; about 4.55 grams of pure gold). This system was inherited by the Byzantine empire and copied by the western barbaric rulers. For centuries after the reform the Byzantine solidus (also called Nomisma, bezant or, later, hyperperon) continued to be struck regularly and remained the main medium of exchange in both international trade and domestic transactions involving large sums, enjoying an incomparable prestige throughout the Mediterranean area. Silver and copper coins continued to be used in local and petty trade. In the west the social and economic disturbances that allowed the barbaric invasions progressively disrupted the monetary system inherited from Rome. The economy shifted toward natural domestic economy where monetary units were increasingly used as units of account rather than means of payment.

The appearance of the Moslems in the Mediterranean did not immediately produce a change in the monetary situation. In the early period of their expansion they continued to use Byzantine and Persian coins. Caliph Adb-el-Malek established an independent Moslem bimetallic monetary system whose two basic Europe the emission of a coinage in gold became common and were the silver dirhem and the gold dinar which broke the monopoly of the Byzantine solidus in the Mediterranean and even gained in prestige outside the Moslem border.

From this period there were three monetary areas: the Byzantine, the Moslem and the western European, which was in a state of general disorganization. An important step in restoring order in the monetary affairs of western Europe was a set of reforms launched by the Carolingians. In their final case, these reforms consisted of the establishment of silver monometallism, the increase of the pound-weight from about 325 to about 410 grams and the adoption of a new monetary unit, called, after the old Roman denarius. The latter was a silver penny, 240 of which were cut from a pound-weight of silver (one penny contained about 1.7 grams of silver). For roughly three centuries the penny remained the only official denomination coined by western mints. Since the Roman era prices and debts had usually been expressed in terms of solidi (shillings), which were still the unit of account at the time of the Carolingian reforms. In the final stage of these reforms it was determined that the solidus was to be equivalent to 12 of the new monetary units (penny). The relationship, therefore, of 1 libra - 20 solidi - 240 denari emerged: these equivalents were to remain the basis of the European monetary system until the French Revolution. Of the three elements, only the penny was an actual coin when the reform was introduced; shilling referred to an old coin no longer in use; and the pound was simply a measure of weight. However, the use of only one denomination proved cumbersome and people began to use the equivalents I: 20 :240 for reckoning.

From the <u>8th century</u>, apart from a few unimportant exceptions, the west did not strike gold coins. The only gold pieces used in international trade were the Moslem dinar and the

Byzantine solidus. Both gold coins displayed an extraordinary ability to remain intrinsically stable in their weight and fineness until the beginning of the <u>11th century</u>: other   coins   did   not display similar long-run stability. In a manner of speaking, in each of the two empires, Moslem and Byzantine, two monetary systems coexisted side by side: one, of considerable stability, based on gold coins and used for international transactions; the other, unstable, based on silver and other metals.

The universal law that seems to make every unit of money lose its value with the passage of time worked throughout the Middle Ages. The progressive lowering of the value of currency took in practice the form of debasement; i.e., reduction in either weight or fineness of coins or both. Debasement was particularly frequent and intense in the case of silver coins, but it did not proceed at the same rate in the various counties: in some it was rather violent and considerable; in others mild and slow. The penny, which originally had been the same throughout Europe, eventually acquired different values in the various regions. The continuous and uneven debasement of the penny meant a reduction in the value of its abstract accounting multiples, shillings and pounds.

For many generations economists and historians interpreted currency debasement as a case of royal falsification of money, clipping or wearing of coins; however, a more complex set of factors must be sought to explain the secular debasement of currency. Among these are long-run increases in the demand for money in the face of relatively inelastic supplies of precious metals, pressures of entrepreneurial groups, deficits in the balance of payments and budgetary deficits.

With the long-term economic expansion in Europe a monetary system of virtually only one local denomination, itself plagued by constant debasement, was becoming increasingly unwieldy and impractical: a need for larger denominations arose. In the 12th century. Venice issued a coin worth 24 pennies; in 1252 Genoa and Florence coined a gold piece. The gold coins of Florence (iorino) and Genoa (genoino) represented a piece of pure gold of the weight of 3.53 grams. The example was quickly taken up by the other Italian and European states and from the middle of the 13 century to the end of the Middle Ages the fiorino and the Venetian ducato enjoyed the highest reputation: they became the international currencies par excellence. Throughout western Europe the emission of a coinage in gold became common and with it the monometallism inaugurated by the Carolingians was finally ended.

Generally speaking, the gold coins of Byzantium and the Moslem empire, and later the gold coins of western Europe, were used as international currencies. Every effort was made to maintain their fineness and weight, yet the fact that they remained generally stable while the silver pieces were progressively debased complicated the monetary structure of many countries. This created social conflicts and the problems of so-called international exchange rate movements that represented one of the tangled aspects of monetary policy in the Middle Ages.

In order to evaluate the economic implications of secular debasement it should be stressed that debasement did not necessarily coincide with inflation. Throughout the Middle Ages the supply of silver and gold was quite inelastic, causing deflationary pressures that were partly offset by the debasements of silver coins. In point of fact, prices expressed in local currencies did not generally increase proportionately (reciprocally) to the debasement of the currencies themselves. Toward the end of the 15th century, discoveries of great silver deposits in Saxony,

Bohemia and Tyrol permitted an increase in the supply of big silver coins. In particular, the testoni and the thaler were introduced. Testoni were first struck in <u>Milan and Venice</u>: thalers in St. Joachimsthal in <u>Bohemia</u> in 1519.

Aside from metallic currency the monetary systems of the Middle Ages included bank money or circulating credit. Credit developed considerably after the 11th century, especially in the Italian trading centers; there, early developments in banking practices and the letter of exchange made credit an important monetary medium. Transfer banks (<u>banchi di scritta</u>) were in operation in the centers of international trade (Constantinople, Venice, Genoa, Florence and Bruges) to facilitate payments through transfer orders. Although the refinement of banking techniques made great progress, quantitatively the most important kind of credit involved delayed payments. This type of transaction allowed a more efficient use of the stock of metallic money and enjoyed a widespread diffusion in the Middle Ages.

8T. THOMAS

The most famous city m the Caribbean and capital of the islands, is named after the consort of King Christian V. 1646-1699-

Fort Christian is the oldest structure in the islands.

CHAPTER III

CHAPTER III
The History of "Paper" Money

Paper Money - History

Though paper media representing gold or other intrinsic-value stores of wealth have been issued in the United States and its predecessor colonies and territories since 1690. the widespread acceptance of paper currency by the American people is a comparatively recent development and came only grudgingly. Paper money emissions by the British colonies in New England, the earliest paper currency within the borders of what is now the United States   of America (U.S.A.) circulated alongside other untraditional exchange media such as Indian wampum shells and musket balls during chronic periods of shortages of "real" - coined - money. Even though the first issues of an organized central government, the Continental Congress' currency notes, promised to pay the bearer face value in "Spanish milled dollars, or the value thereof in gold or silver," these notes circulated at a heavy discount - if they were acceptable at ALL. The fledgling government's final solution for the Continental Currency
problem, accepting them in 1787 at 1% of face value in exchange for interest bearing bonds, did nothing to bolster public confidence in paper money.

Neither did the often larcenous "banking" practices of the various elements of the private sector to whom the note-issuing prerogative fell. With states denied the power to issue money by the Constitution of the United States, and the powers of the Federal Government to   do   so   left unspecified; various private issues of banks, railroads, utilities, and even individual citizens, cropped up, with varying resources to guarantee their value, until the Government halted the practice in 1863. By the late 19th Century. U.S.-issued paper money had become a viable pat of the nation's commerce as people recognized that such notes were, indeed, redeemable on demand for gold or silver. By 1963. paper currency was such an ingrained part of the American

28

economy that the Government was able to remove all specie-redemption quality from its currency issues, raising only minimal objections from strict interpretationists of the Constitution. Now, ironically, paper money may be on the way out as a circulating medium of exchange. The growth of demand deposits (checking accounts), electronic fund transfers and the arrival of the home computer age may one day soon put an end for the need for physical symbols of wealth to pass from hand to hand.

History of Pre-Federal Paper Money in the U.S.

To better understand the forces which shaped the United States Government's issues of paper currency since 1861. it is necessary to look backward to the many and varied public and private currency issues which preceded them in this country. The use of paper money in the area which would become the United States of America actually predates its use in many parts of Western Europe and in most of the rest of the world. While paper currencies had been in use in China since the 7th Century, when it was known as "flying money" because of its light weight and ability to circulate widely with ease, it was not until the late 17th Century that the western world began experiments with non. metallic circulating currencies. Surprisingly quickly, the North American continent had its first "paper money" issues in 1685. when the Intendant of New France (Canada) issued promissory notes hand-printed on pieces of playing cards, to circulate as money until the delayed arrival of the paymaster. The Massachusetts Bay Colony followed suit soon after, issuing in December, 1690. f7,000 worth of the first publicly authorized paper money notes in the western world to pay expenses of a border war with Canada (previous paper money issues in Europe and North America had been either issued by banks, or were emergency measures not authorized by any public body). Following that precedent, by the turn of the 18th Century, other colonies were emitting paper currencies as needed to run their specie-short economies. By the end of the War for Independence. All 13 colonies had issued some form of paper currency. Beginning in May, 1775. the Congress of the newly unified former colonies began the issue of Continental Currency to finance its fight for freedom.

The Continental Currency was plagued, though, by increasing public distrust. The Continental paper dollar was able to hold its value at par with a specie dollar only until October, 1777. by which time widespread counterfeiting by British, Tories and opportunists conspired with the natural inflation of a printing press economy and increasing uncertainty as to the outcome of the war to push the exchange ratio of the Continental Currency to $11 in paper for $10 in specie. After that point, the devaluation accelerated. By the next year. October, 1778. the ratio was 4.66 to 1. The low point was reached in April, 1780, when a dollar in silver or gold was worth $40 Continental. And these were the official exchange ratios adopted by the Congress and many of the states, to offset the rampant inflation. In actual commerce, the Continentals were all but worthless. George Washington himself lamented that it took a wagon full of Continental Currency to purchase a wagon load of supplies for his army. A truer measure of the value of the Government paper currency could be found in the fact that by October, 1787. amid speculation that the Continental Currency might never be redeemable, it was selling at the rate of $250 paper for $1 specie (coin). Eventually the Government issued 6% interest bearing bonds at the rate of $1 for every $100 of Continental Currency turned in. Issued current with the Colonial and Continental currencies were numerous privately-sponsored paper monies

29

emitted by banks (as early as <u>1732</u> in Connecticut), utilities, merchants, individuals and even churches. These issues continued after the Revolutionary War. and proliferated in the <u>19th Century</u>. Today, lumped together under the generic, if not altogether correct, label of "broken bank notes." these colorful, historic notes and their collectible adjuncts make up a significant portion of the paper money hobby's interest.

The tens of thousands of privately-issued bank and scrip notes of the <u>1800s</u> ranged in denomination from one-half cent to several thousand dollars. While today their collector value depends on a combination of rarity, condition and demand; their value when issued was solely dependent on the reputation of the issuing authority - be it bank, railroad or Main   Street apothecaries. In those days, when a note, might be worth every cent of its face value or might be worth nothing more than the paper on which it was printed, an entire industry sprang up to supply banks and merchants with accurate, timely information about which notes would pass current, which should be accepted only at a discount, and those from an issuer who had gone "broken." In addition, because of the wealth of larcenous talent available for changing broken bank notes into "good" notes through the alteration of a bank   or   city   name,   or   raising   the denomination of a note from $1 to $10 by deft penmanship; those who handled the dizzying variety of paper money in circulation in the mid <u>19th Century</u> needed books which listed and described the genuine issues of a particular bank. (It is. incidentally, from the common name of these paper money reporting services that the name Bank Note Reporter was derived for the monthly paper money newspaper published by the publisher of this catalog.) The only restraints on the issue of paper money at that time were those which the individual states cared to apply, and such restraints were infrequent and ineffective. The Federal Government put an effective end to these halcyon days of currency free-for-all   in   <u>1863</u>.   by   imposing   a   10%   tax   on   out¬ standing notes; and later through the 14th <u>Amendment</u> to the Constitution, forbidding the private issue of circulating media of exchange altogether. With that the Government of the United States of America attained a monopoly on the note-issuing function which it has maintained, except in localized emergency situations, to this day.

<u>Large Size Notes</u>
Brief and basically historical backgrounds have been provided for each of the major types of U.S. Currency. No great amount of fiscal or legislative data has been provided, except where it might serve to clarify some aspects of the notes themselves or their collectability.

<u>Demand Notes</u>

Despite two issues of interest-bearing Treasury notes in <u>1860-1861</u>. the opening guns of the Civil War found the United States Government shot of the necessary funds to put down the rebellion in a protracted war. Congress moved swiftly in the national emergency to   provide legislation authorizing the issue of $60,000,000 by Acts of July 17, and Aug. 5, <u>1861</u>. It is generally believed among numismatists today that the Demand Notes were backed by faith in the Government alone; but this was not entirely the case. By the terms of the authorizing legislation, the Demand Notes were not payable in gold. But, in a circular from the Secretary of the Treasury sent out before the suspension of specie payments on Dec. 21, <u>1861</u>. they were declared payable in coin, and the Government redeemed them as such in order to sustain its credit. Thus, for a short time in 1861, the Demand Notes were quoted on a par with gold.

However, as the war progressed, in most parts of the country the Demand Notes - and all other paper money of the U.S. Government - were acceptable only at a discount, even though they were receivable for all payments to the Government, including duties.

The Demand Notes took their famous "Greenback" nickname from the color of their back designs (back designs in themselves were scarce on paper money in the U.S. prior to the Civil War). The name was subsequently applied to virtually every other form of U.S. currency and remains current today. Because the United States Government was not prepared to be in the note-printing business in 1861, the work of producing the Demand Notes was contracted to the American Bank Note Company and National Bank Note Company. Working with essentially stock currency elements, the private contractors turned out more than 7.25 million $5, $10 and $20 Demand Notes. The actual "issuing" of the notes required that they be signed by the treasurer of the United States (Changes) and the Register of the Treasury (Changes), or persons designated by them.

Accordingly, platoons of clerks within the Treasury Department were put to work autographing Demand Notes. However, on the very earliest specimens, the engraved blanks on the face of the notes indicated only the office of the signer, and the clerks were required to pen in the words "for the" on each note as they signed it, a most laborious process that was eliminated with the addition of "for the" on the engraved face plates themselves. The Demand Notes which survive today with the hand-signed "for the" on the face are much scarcer than the engraved version, and command a significant price premium. Rarity and value of the Demand Notes is also affected by the engraved location on the face of the note indicating where the notes were issued and, therefore, payable. The obligation on the notes reads: "The United States promises to pay to the bearer five dollars (or ten dollars or twenty dollars) on demand. . . payable by the Assistant Treasurer of the United States at..." One of five cities was then engraved. Those notes payable at New York are far and away the most common among the survivors, with Philadelphia second and Boston third. Specimens which promise redemption in Cincinnati and, especially, St. Louis, are extremely rare and seldom encountered.

United States Notes (Legal Tender Note)

The longest - Lived type of U.S. paper money, the United States Notes (called interchangeably Legal Tender Notes because of the wording of the obligation) was first authorized in 1862 and is still current today, though none have been issued since 1969. The subject of major Constitutional debate at the time of their issue, the notes did much to pave the way for future issues of U.S. currency backed only by the credit of the Government. While there are five official "issues" of large size Legal Tender Notes, as well as the small size series, they are generally collected today by type (major design) and, occasionally, by signature combination. The First Issue of United States Notes, dated March 10, 1862. was issued in denominations of $5, $10, $20, $50, $100, $500 and $1,000. Two different varieties of notes, bearing different obligation wording on the backs, are popularly collected among the First Issue notes. The earliest First Issues bear what is known as the First Obligation on back, reading: "This note is a legal tender for all debts, public and private, except duties on imports and interest on the public debt, and is exchangeable for U.S. six per cent twenty year bonds, redeemable at the pleasure of the United States after five years." The Second Obligation, much rarer, reads as follows: "This

31

note is a legal tender for all debts, public and private, except duties on imports and interest on the public debt, and is receivable in payment of all loans made to the United States."

These First Issue notes do not carry the large face inscriptions "United States Note" or "Treasury Note," which are found on later Legal Tender issues. Dated Aug. I, 1862. and issued only in denominations of $1 and $2, the Second Issue U.S. Notes carry the Second Obligation on back. The Third Issue U.S. Notes, dated March 10, 1863, were issued in denominations from $5 through $1,000, again using the Second Obligation. Fourth Issue Legal   Tenders   were authorized by an Act of Congress dated March 3, 1863. and issued in denomination from $1 through $10,000 in the various Series of 1869,1874,1878,1880,1907,1917 and 1923. Those
notes in Series 1869 bear the label "Treasury Notes" on face, with all later issues carrying the "United States Notes" designation. Back obligation on all series is the same: "This note is a legal tender at its face value for all debts public and private, except duties on imports and
interest on the public debt." The Fifth Issue Legal Tenders consisted solely of the Series 1901 $10 note (the popular Bison design), issued under the authority of the Legal Tender Acts   of
1862-1863. A new face obligation was introduced: "This note is a legal tender for ten dollars subject to the provisions of Section 3588 R.S.," on back, the obligation reads: "This note is a legal tender at its face value for all debts public and private except duties on imports   and
interest on the public debt."

Legislation remains in force requiring that the amount of Legal Tender Notes in official circulation be maintained at $346,681.016. which is done, on paper at least, through the continuing "circulation" of the small size Red Seal $100s.

Compound Interest Treasury Notes
Circulating currency notes which grew In face value each six-month period they remained in circulation were just one of the innovations to which the Federal Government turned to finance the protracted Civil War. Authorized by Congressional Acts of March 3, 1863, and June 30, 1864, these notes were intended to circulate for three years, bearing interest at the then-
attractive rate of six percent a year, compounded semi-annually. The backs of each note carry a table spelling out the actual interest earned and current face value of the note through maturity. Theoretically, a note that was acquired when issued at face value, could be spent a year later as $10.60; although little is known as to whether this theory worked in   practice.   It   is   known,
though, that those persons holding the notes at maturity generally took their profit, leaving very few surviving specimens for today's collectors. Neither should it be assumed that the surviving notes continue to earn interest. The interest payments ended at maturity (if interest had been allowed to accumulate, the $10 note, as of June, 1985. would have a "face value" in excess of $11,000 - even more than the numismatic value of the note - with corresponding denominations
- $20, $50, $100, $500 and $1,000 - worth multiples thereof).

The face of each note bears a surcharge in large gold letters, reading "Compound Interest

Treasury Note," along with corresponding numerals of issue value. Unfortunately, the gold ink used for these overprints contributed greatly to the demise of the notes themselves, for it is highly acidic and attacks the rather fragile paper to the point where many examples are found with this surcharge "burned" into and through the paper. Additionally, the $50 and $100 notes,

the highest values which could practically be said to have circulated, were extensively counterfeited and the Treasury was forced to withdraw them in the face of such "competition." In any denomination, the Compound Interest Treasury Notes are scarce in better   than   Fine condition. Examples are known with a number of different issue dates on face. The $10-$50 notes with the June 10 or July 15, 1864, dates are the rarest, with dates from Aug. 15, 1864, through Oct. 16, 1865, being more common; while in the $100 notes, the June 10, 1864, date is most common, followed by the Aug. 15, 1864-Sept. 1, 1865, dates. No July 15,   1864-dated $ 100 Compound Interest Treasury Notes are known, nor are there any reported survivors among the $500 and $1,000 denominations, though the Treasury repots several examples still
officially outstanding.

Interest Bearing Notes

As a group, probably the rarest type of U.S. paper money is the Interest Bearing Note issues of the Civil War era. Like the Compound Interest Treasury Notes and the Refunding Certificates (also interest bearing), they were something of a desperation currency issue by the   Federal Government to bolster the Union war chest. The Interest Bearing Notes were issued in a trio of distinctive types, all of which are very rare, or unknown to have survived. The first issue was a series of One-Year Notes, issued under authority of the Act of March 3. 1863. and   paying interest of five percent for one year. Face designs of the one-year issue were similar to the Compound Interest Treasury Notes, without the gold surcharges. Backs were significantly different, lacking the tabular interest-figuring chart. A face inscription reads: "One year after date the United States will pay to the bearer with five per interest - dollars." On back,   the obligation was worded: "This note is a legal tender at its face value, excluding interest, for all debts public and private, except duties on imports and interest on the public debt." Denominations of the One-Year Notes ranged from $10 through $5,000, with no specimens of the $500, $1,000 or $5,000 known. Each note bears an individually stamped date of issue on the face. One year from that date, the notes were redeemable for face value plus interest. Two Year Notes were also authorized by the March 3. 1863 Act of Congress. Issued only in the $50, $100, $500 and $1,000 denominations, and paying five percent interest per year for a two-year term, they are naturally much scarcer because of the high return they offered the holder near the end of the Civil War. Designs were completely different from the One- Year Notes, although the face and back inscriptions are similar.

Like the Interest Bearing Notes themselves, the Three- Year Notes are comprised of three separate issues, due to three different authorizing Acts of Congress; July 17. 1861. June 30, 1864. and March 3, 1865. Again issued in the higher denominations, from $50 through $5,000, the notes paid interest at the rate of 7 -3/10 percent a year; the highest rate the Government paid on circulating notes. Like the Compound Interest Treasury Notes, the actual amount of interest is spelled out on the notes, though in this case it is expressed in terms of interest per day. Thus, the $50 note expresses a promise to pay interest of one cent per day, while the $5,000 bill paid interest at the rate of $1 per day. That the notes were not intended to circulate widely is indicated by the fact that they are payable to the order, not to the bearer. That is, there is a blank on the face of every Three-Year Interest Bearing Note for the name of the original holder, and a corresponding blank on back for endorsement at the time of maturity. Another feature which makes the Three-Year Notes unusual among U.S. paper money issues was the original attachment of five coupons to each note. Each coupon indicated the interest payable for a six month period, and was removed from the note when that interest was collected semi-annually. The final interest payment was made when the note itself was presented for redemption at the end of the three-year period. This arrangement is spelled out on the face of each note.

As mentioned earlier, these notes are of the greatest rarity, most of them unknown to survive, existing only in proof form or existing in a unique, or nearly so, issued example.

Refunding Certificates

More of a government security than circulating medium of exchange, the Refunding Certificates authorized by Congress in the Act of Feb. 26. 1879. brought these interest bearing instruments within the reach of more Americans in that they were denominated at $10. The authorizing legislation intended that these notes bear interest of four percent annually in perpetuity. However, in 1907 Congress passed a law stopping interest payments as of July I, forever fixing the "face" value of these notes at $21.30. Presumably at that time the incentive for the public to hold these notes was removed, and their redemption accelerated. The $10 Refunding Certificates were issued in two different forms, one type payable to the bearer, the other to the order of the original purchaser. Like the Three-Year Interest Bearing Notes, the Refunding Certificates payable to order had spaces on face and back for the owner and endorser. The "pay to order" type is far rarer than the "pay to bearer" variety Rather than being redeemable for specie, per se, these notes, in amounts of $50 or more, were convertible into four percent bonds.

Silver Certificates

Among the most popular of U.S. notes due to their wealth of design excellence and challenging, but not impossible, rarity, the Silver Certificates of 1878-1963 comprise five major issues of large size notes, and the various series of small size notes. Authorizing legislation for all issues were the Congressional Act of Feb. 28, 1878, and Aug. 4, 1886. The First Issue Silver Certificates consist of Series 1878 and 1880 notes in denominations from $10-$1,000. The notes of 1878, besides bearing the engraved signatures of GW Scoield, Register of the Treasury, and James Gilillan, Treasurer of the U.S., have on their face an engraved or autographed countersignature of the Assistant Treasurers in New York, Washington, D.C., and San Francisco, attesting that the requisite amount of silver dollars had been deposited in their offices to cover the face value of the notes. In addition to the Series 1878 countersigned notes, several $20 Series 1880 Silver Certificates are known bearing the engraved countersignature of T. Hillhouse, Assistant Treasurer at New York. The silver bills' Second Issue was made up of notes from $1 through $1,000 in the Series of 1886, 1891 and 1908, although not all denominations were issued in all series. The "Educational" notes, $1, $2, and $5 Silver Certificates of Series 1896. are the sole component of the Third Issue.

Similarly, the Fourth Issue Silver Certificates are made up of $1, $2 and $5 notes of the Series of 1899. The Silver Certificates of the Fifth Issue are the Series 1923 $1 and $5 notes. The obligation on the First Issue notes reads: "This certifies that there have been deposited with the Treasurer of the U.S. at Washington, D.C. (or Assistant Treasurers at New York and San Francisco) payable at his office to the bearer on demand - silver dollars. This certificate is receivable for customs, taxes and all public dues and when so received may be reissued." Obligation on the last four issues of silver notes was worded: "This certifies that there have been deposited in the Treasury of the United States - silver dollars payable to the bearer on demand. This certificate is receivable for customs, taxes and all public dues and when so received may be issued."

Treasury or Coin Notes

Pushed through Congress by the silver mining industry, the authorizing legislation of July 14, 1890. which created the Treasury Notes carefully did not specify that they be redeemable in silver; only that they be issued to pay for silver bullion purchased by the Treasury and that they be payable "in Coin" (hence the more commonly encountered name Coin Notes). With the co¬ operation of Treasury officials, silver sellers were able to turn their bullion in at artificially high official prices, receive the Coin Notes in payment, and redeem them immediately for gold coin and a tidy profit. In denominations of $1, $2, $5, $10, $20, $100 and $1,000, the Coin Notes were issued in Series 1890 and 1891 form, the 1890 issue bearing ornately engraved green back designs that filled the print area. The $50 was issued only in Series of 1891, and the $500 note, which had been designed and a plate prepared with the portrait of Gen. William T. Sherman, was not issued at all. It was felt that even as late as 25 years after the Civil War, the use of Sherman's portrait on a currency note would inflame passions in the South. The 1890 notes are much scarcer and in greater demand than the Series 1891 issue, especially in new condition. Face and back obligations of the Coin Notes are interesting and unique. They read: "This United States of America will pay to bearer - dollars in coin." And, "This note is a legal tender at its face value in payment of all debts public and private except when otherwise expressly stipulated in the contract."

National Gold Bank Notes

Gold and the American West have been inseparably linked as part of this nation's history since the discovery of gold at Sutter's Mill in 1848. The unique, but short-lived National Gold Bank Note series was a contemporary part of "The Golden West," and today trades on that romantic image - and the inherent rarity of the notes themselves as one of the most sought-after types of U.S. paper money.

The National Gold Bank Notes were authorized under the provisions of the Currency Act of July 12. 1870. and are very much analogous to the regular National Currency issue. The principal difference, besides design, is that the National Gold Bank Notes were payable - and prominently said so - in gold coin. This was a concession to the traditional mistrust of Western America in paper currency and the Californian area's long history of gold use as the principal medium of exchange, whether in the form of gold dust, nuggets, private-issue coinage or genuine coins of the United States Mint. Under the general provisions of the National Bank Act of 1863, the National Gold Banks had to secure the issue of their currency with the deposit of bonds with the Treasurer of the United States. However, the conditions for the N.GB.N. issues were a bit more stringent. The Gold Banks could issue notes only to the value of 80% of their deposited bonds, while the other National banks could issue to 90%. Additionally, the Gold Banks were required to have on hand in their vaults gold coinage equal to 25% of the value of their note issue. The responsibility of redeeming these notes in gold, lay with the issuing banks, not the Federal Government, which did not resume specie payments until 1879, nearly a decade after the N.GB.N. issues began. The Treasury would, of course, redeem National Gold Bank Notes for other lawful currency.

This gold redemption property gave the N.GB.Ns, the necessary credibility, and they circulated at par with the precious metal. They circulated so extensively that surviving notes are generally found in conditions which many collectors would find unacceptable in other   U.S.   currency types. No strictly uncirculated National Gold Bank Note is known today, and the average condition found is Good to Very Good. Specimens in Fine or better condition command attractive premiums in the infrequent times when they become available. Though authorized in denominations from $5-$ 1,000, National Gold Bank Notes were issued to circulation only as high as $500. The face of each note was similar to corresponding denominations in the First Charter National Bank Note series, while the backs had as their central   feature   a   photo-like engraving of a stack of U.S. gold pieces, representing $211.50 face value in $1 through $20 denominations. In all, 10 National Gold Banks were chartered, nine in California and The Kidder National Gold Bank in Boston, Mass. Notes were actually printed for the Kidder N.GB., and delivered, but the bank eventually returned them all for cancellation, never issuing them to circulation. The Kidder was the only National Gold Bank to have $1,000 notes prepared. Because of the relatively small size of the issue, much can be determined about the issue and survivability of the National Gold Bank Notes. In the period 1870-1878. exactly 196,849 notes, with a face value of $3,267,420, were issued. Treasury records indicate a total of 6,639 notes remain outstanding (including four $500 examples, none of which are known to collectors). A recent comprehensive survey of known notes accounted for fewer than 275 in all denominations.

Like the other National Bank Notes, National Gold Bank Notes are known in both Original Series and Series of 1875 issues, although all nine California banks did not issue   all denominations in both series. Indeed, the Series 1875 notes are somewhat scarcer than the Original notes.

Federal Reserve Bank Notes
Often confused with the Federal Reserve Notes, which are currency issues of the Federal Reserve System itself Federal Reserve Bank Notes were issued by the 12 individual Federal Reserve Banks, much like the National Bank Notes. Indeed, Federal Reserve Bank Notes, large and small size, carry the "National Currency" inscription. In the large size note-issuing period, the similarity of Federal Reserve Bank Notes to Federal Reserve notes extended to nearly identical back designs in the $5-$50 denominations, FRBNs were also issued   in $1   and $2 denominations, while the FRNs were issued in value from $5 through $10,000. Two separate issues of Federal Reserve Bank Notes comprise the large size issue, while there was a single issue in small size. The Series 1915 FRBNs were authorized under the terms of the Federal Reserve Act of December. 23, 1913. Issued only in denominations of $5-$20, only the banks in Atlanta, Chicago, Kansas City, Dallas and San Francisco participated, with the Frisco bank issuing only $5s.

Like the National Bank Notes, the obligation to pay the bearer on the FRBNs is made by the issuing bank, rather than the Fed system or U,S, Government. The security notice on the 1915 issue reads: "Secured by United States bonds deposited with the Treasurer of the United States." That obligation was changed for the Series 1918 FRBNs, issued under authority of a Congressional Act of April 23, 1918, The modification reads: "Secured by United States certificates of indebtedness or United States one-year gold notes, deposited with the Treasurer of the United States." The Series 1918 FRBNs consist of all denominations from $1 through $50, though again, not all 12 banks issued all denominations, For instance, only the Atlanta and St, Louis banks issued $20 Series 1918 FRBNs, while only St. Louis issued $50s. Spurred initially by demand for the attractive "Battleship" back design of the $2, and the defiant eagle on the $1 (symbols of America's defense posture in World War I, all large size FRBNs are actively collected today, especially in New condition. A wealth of combinations of U.S. Government signatures combined with signatures of the various Governors and Cashiers of the individual issuing banks, creates myriad varieties to keep the series challenging.

Also contributing to the challenge is the sheer scarcity of surviving specimens. Treasury sources indicate just over $2 million worth of FRBNs outstanding, from a total issue of more than $760 million.

Federal Reserve Notes
Authorized by the Federal Reserve Act of Dec. 23. 1913 and first issued in 1914, the Federal Reserve Note is the only type of U.S. paper money which continues in production "today." The large size issues of FRNs are in two series, 1914, in denominations from $5-$100, and 1918, in denominations from $500-$10,000. Additionally, two distinctive varieties of 1914 notes exist, those with red Treasury seal and serial number, and those with the elements in blue. The Red Seal 1914 FRNs are considerably scarcer than the blue. While they are issued to circulation through the 12 Federal Reserve Bank's the FRNs are an obligation of the United States Government, rather than bank named thereon (unlike the Federal Reserve Bank Notes). Neither are Federal Reserve Notes secured by government bonds, precious metals or other reserves. The obligation on FRNs simply states that: "The United States of America will pay to the bearer on demand - dollars."

On back, the redemption qualities of the large size FRNs was spelled out thus: "This note is receivable by all National and member banks and Federal Reserve Banks and for all taxes, customs and other public dues. It is redeemable in gold on demand at the Treasury Department of the United States in the city of Washington, District of Columbia or in gold or lawful money at any Federal Reserve Bank." This redeemable-in-gold clause continued in use on the Series 1928 small size FRNs, but was revoked with the passage of the Gold Reserve Act of 1933. The obligation, beginning with the Series 1934 notes, was modified to read: "This note is legal tender for an debts, public and private, and is redeemable in lawful money at the United States Treasury, or at any Federal Reserve Bank." Beginning with Series 1963, the obligation was changed to its present form: "This note is legal tender for all debts, public and private." Wide variances III the number of notes printed for each bank in any particular series of a denomination have created many challenging issues within the Federal Reserve Note series, both large and small size.

37

Gold Certificates

With their bright orange back designs (though some early gold notes are uniface), the large size Gold Certificates issued from 1865 through 1928 are a popular and tangible reminder of the days when U.S. paper currency was "as good as gold."

While many of the earlier Gold Certificate issues were not designed to be used in general circulation, due to their high face value, later types did enter the channels of commerce, circulating alongside the myriad other currency issues of the late 19th and early 20th Centuries. Nine separate issues of Gold Certificates were created in the large size series, several of which were used almost exclusively in inter-bank channels to transfer and settle gold accounts. The first issue gold backs were authorized by the Currency Act of March 3. 1863. and consisted of notes in denominations of $20, $100, $500, $1,000, $5,000 and $10,000. While examples of the two lowest denominations survive, they are extremely rare. No known examples of the second
issue Gold Certificates are known today. Issued pursuant to the same act, and countersigned and dated by hand in the 1870-71 period, they were in denominations of $100 and $10,000 only.

Third issue gold notes, bearing the impression "Series of 1875," were also issued in limited denominations: $100, $500, and $1,000. Uniface, the issue is represented today by only a few examples of the $100 note. With the fourth issue, Gold Certificates entered general circulation, and the type begins to be known by its series designation. Ten-dollar gold backs were issued in Series 1907 and 1922; $20 in Series 1882, 1905,1906 and 1922; $50 in Series 1882, 1913 and 1922; $100 in Series 1882 and 1922; $500 in Series 1882; $1,000 in Series 1882, 1907 and 1922; $5,000 in Series 1882 and 1888; and, $10,000 in Series 1882, 1888 and 1900. Naturally, the notes in denominations above $100 are very rare, though not unknown. To correspond the various issues to the series in these post-1875 notes; the fourth issue consisted of the Series 1882 notes; the fifth issue comprises the 1888 Series, the sixth is the 1900 $10,000 notes; the
seventh issue Gold Certificates are the Series 1905, 1906 and 1907 $10 and $20 notes; the eighth is the $1,000 of Series 1907; and, the ninth issue of large size Gold Certificates are the Series 1913 ($50 only) and 1922 gold backs in $10-$1,000 denominations.

The Dollar Decoded

CHAPTER IV

BANKS AND BANKING

Drawn and engraved (1798-1800) by W. Birch and Son; The New York Public Library, The I.N. Phelps Stokes Collection of American Historical Prints.

The Frist Bank of the United States, established in 1791, had its later headquarters in this building in Philadelphia.

CHAPTER IV
The History of Banking

The following general survey of banking is divided into three main sections: (I) history; (II) principles of banking; and (III) practice of banking. The first section in turn is divided into three subsections: (A) the history of ancient, medieval and continental European banking; (B) the history of banking in Great Britain and the commonwealth; and (C) United States banking history.

L HISTORY OF BANKING

In considering the history of banking we must distinguish between central banks and commercial banks. The essential functions of a central bank are to act as bankers' bank, lender of last resort and regulator of monetary and debit conditions in the country in which it operates; most central banks also act as government bankers and many have a monopoly of note issue. The commercial bank makes loans and provides a means of payment by transfer of deposits from one account to another, but its most distinctive and significant feature is its power to create credit by lending sums larger than those which have been deposited in actual cash with it. These functions are common to all fully developed commercial banks; some have also engaged in other activities including note issue, dealing in foreign currencies, acceptance and discount of bills of exchange and the issue of loans for governments or private industry. Our definition, however, excludes savings banks (q.v.), investment banks and other institutions the primary purpose of which is not the acceptance of deposits, and the creation of credit; these will be mentioned only incidentally. Central banking is of comparatively late growth, but commercial banking began to evolve in the later middle ages from the much older functions of moneylending and currency dealing.

A. ANCIENT. MEDIEVAL AND CONTINENTAL EUROPEAN

Origins

There are records of loans by the temples of Babylon as early as 2.000 B.C.: and c. 575 B.C. a private firm, the Igibi bank, was making loans and receiving deposits, at interest. In Greece by the 4th century B.C. financial activities, were being performed by the temples, by public bodies and by private: firms. The latter accepted deposits, made loans, tested and changed coins and arranged credit transactions between cities to avoid the movement of specie (Heavy Coin). The Greek system was, imported into Hellenistic Egypt and also influenced Rome. Roman law recognized payment in bank in discharge of a debt, and in, the 2nd century, A.D. public notaries were appointed to register such transaction. The decline of trade after the breakup of the Roman empire made banking facilities less necessary, and usury laws imposed restraints on lending. Records from Genoa and other Italian cities go back to the 12th century, but it is not until the 14th century that a large volume of evidence is available. By this time the trade of Europe had developed along two main lines; (I:) the Italian cities and, later, Bruges, Antwerp and the towns of the Hanseatic league became centers of warehouse trade and developed local banking systems; and (2) at certain centers of communications there grew up the great international

fairs, of which those of Champagne are the most famous, with their own system of finance through ambulatory bankers and also their function as centers for international clearings. Distinct from both these systems, though participating at times in the activities of both, were the international financiers concerned, among other things, with the finance of the international wool trade with the collection and transmission of papal revenues and with loans to kings and princes.

When deposit banking re-emerged in medieval Europe, the only way of transferring bank credit was through oral instruction by the debtor and acceptance by the creditor in the presence of wit¬ nesses. Holograph documents (written in the hand of the principal) came into use in the 13th and 14th centuries, and by the second half of the 14th the nonnegotiable bill of exchange was firmly established. But the use of any document serving the purpose of the modern check was only occasional before 1500, and the legal doctrine of negotiability evolved only gradually from the 16th to the 18th centuries. At the Champagne fairs the value of purchases appears to have been recorded in the books of a fair banker as they were made. At the end of the fair the various book debts were offset, so far as possible, against one another, and balances settled either in cash or by drawing a bill payable at the next fair. By the 15th century the fairs were also serving as clearinghouses for payments arising in other forms of trade; for example, the Cely family in England was taking bills payable at the fairs in payment for wool exported through the Calais staple; and similar methods seem to have been used at the other important fairs. The system, though ingenious and highly important in its day, involved neither deposits nor credit creation, so that it did not contribute much to the evolution of modern banking.

The same might be said of, the great merchant bankers who dominated high finance during the, middle ages and the Renaissance. The men of Piacenza were the first Christian bankers to challenge monopoly of the Jews in this field. They were soon displaced by others from Siena, Lucca and Florence, but the name of Lombard clung to them all. The Bardi and Peruzzi of Florence and the Frescobaldi of Lucca played a big part in the state finances both of England and France, but their power was broken by Edward Ill's repudiation of his debts in 1339 followed by the confiscation of their property in France and by a revolution in Florence. Native financiers such as William de la Pole in England and Jacque Coeur in France were unable for long to meet the growing needs of their governments, and the 15th century saw a second period of Florentine financial power. This time the outstanding family was that of the Medici, who laid the foundations of their immense fortune as financial agents for the papacy. The Florentines suffered again from defaults and confiscations and gradually lost ground to Genoese and Germans. One other name must be mentioned, that of the Fugger, who were the greatest moneylenders of the 16th century: they played a vital part in the election of Charles V as emperor and supported him through all the vicissitudes of his reign and also had extensive dealings in Germany, Italy, Hungary, Spain, the Netherlands and England. However, they too suffered the common fate of their kind, meeting their ruin in the crash of the Spanish state finances at the end of the 16th century. These and other smaller firms dealt to some extent in borrowed money though they relied largely upon their own capital; they had little interest in ordinary commercial finance and were agents for raising of government loans and the management of the resulting exchange transactions rather than bankers in the modern sense.

The sedentary bankers of the Mediterranean cities, especially Venice, Genoa and Barcelona, were the <u>direct ancestors</u> of modem commercial bankers. They accepted deposits which were regularly transferred from one account to another in payment for commercial debts; the normal method of transfer was by an entry inscribed by the banker in his books in the presence of both debtor and creditor. In the 14th and 15th centuries Venetian bankers allowed customers to overdraw their accounts, but this was regarded as an abuse. Failures among them were common, and as early as 1356 there were proposals for the establishment of a public bank. It was not until 1587, however, that the Banco della Piazza di Rialto was founded. It was to receive deposits in coin, to transfer them from one account o another and to pay bills of exchange, but it was not to make loans nor, since it had no legal source of revenue, did it pay interest on deposits. Its services were performed free, expenses being a charge on the state. The constitution was not strictly observed, and the bank did make loans, especially to the government, and got into difficulties as a result. It was to meet the difficulties of the state that the Banco Giro was formed in 1619, the creditors of the government agreeing to accept payment in the form of credits with the new bank. The two public banks were fused in 1638 and continued to operate until 1806. Other important public banks dating from the middle ages were the Casa di San Giorgio in Genoa (1148) and the Bank of Deposit in Barcelona (1401).

<u>The Bank of Amsterdam</u>, founded in 1609, was similar in constitution to the Banco della Piazza di Rialto. Its original functions were to accept and transfer deposits, to exchange coins, to purchase current and incurrent coin for the mint and to act as a clearinghouse for bills of exchange. All bills of more than 600 florins were to be made payable at the bank, but this law was not strictly enforced. The overdrawing of accounts was prohibited, but the bank did give credit to certain institutions, including the city of Amsterdam and the Dutch East India company. By the beginning of the 18th century bank deposits had become inconvertible, but for many years they circulated freely and the bank maintained their value by prudent management. However, it suffered severely in the French wars at the end of the 18th century and was liquidated in 1819. Similar Giro banks were founded in other Dutch cities and, in 1619, at Hamburg.

<u>The 18th and 19th Centuries</u>—France—At the beginning of the 18th century, when banking in England was making rapid progress, France suffered from the failure of the financial system of John Law (q.v.). The Banque Generale was founded in 1716 as a bank of deposit and also of note issue, but its constitution provided that notes were to be issued only against the deposit of coin and that no credit was to be given to private customers. However, the bank soon became involved with the rest of the "system" and these principles were disregarded. In 1717 the Compagnie d'Occident was formed to trade with Louisiana, and two years later it was

transformed into, the Compagnie des Indes, with a monopoly of foreign trade and the right to farm the customs; Law now proposed to repay the public debt by making the creditors of the state into shareholders in the company. In 1718 the bank, then known as the Banque Royale, had its notes made legal tender. It became more and more involved with the company, issuing a great volume of notes in order to support the value of the company's shares in the market. These reckless issues helped to produce a violent inflation and to bring about the collapse of the "system" in 1720. The holders of Law's notes lost heavily and the idea of a note issuing bank was discredited in France for many years to come.

A number of banks doing discount and' deposit business were founded during the 18th century, but there was no bank of issue until 1776. Then Blanchaud (a Swiss) and Clouard (a   Scot) formed the Caisse d'Escompte, which made overgenerous advances to the government and was liquidated in 1793. In 1796 a syndicate of private bankers in Paris founded the Caisse   des Comptes Courants, and shortly afterward the Caisse d'Escompte de Commerce was formed by a commercial group. Both were taken over by the Bank of France in 1800 and 1803, respectively.

The Bank of France was founded in 1800 and received its basic constitution In laws Of 1800, 1803, 1806 and 1808. The management was entrusted to a governor and 2 deputy governors appointed by the head of the state and a council of 15 regents and 3 auditors elected   by   the general assembly of the 200 largest shareholders. The business 'of the bank was to be note issue, receipt of deposits on current account, collection and discount of bills of exchange and dealing in precious metals. It also acted as banker to the state and was at times called upon   to   make large advances to the government. In 1803 the bank was given a monopoly of note issue in Paris. A number of provincial banks of issue were founded under the July monarchy, but all their notes were discredited during the 1848 revolution, and the Bank of France arranged amalgamations with them. Thenceforward (apart from a brief interval in which other notes circulated in Savoy after its cession to France) the Bank of France was the sole issuing body. There was no legal requirement of a reserve. A maximum issue was fixed by law, but   the restriction had little meaning: in times of difficulty the bank always asked for and obtained an increased issue. Notes were made legal, tender and inconvertible in 1870, but full convertibility was restored in 1878. The law of 1808 empowered the bank to establish branches, and several were set up between 1830 and 1840. Under a law of 1857 the bank could be compelled to set up at least one branch in each department, and at the end of the century about 120 branches had been established.

For many years the Bank of France was practically the only institution offering facilities for the transfer of current-account balances. The check was little used and was not fully recognized in French law until 1865. Hence, the circulation both of notes and of bills of exchange was much greater than in England. The bank discounted very small bills, but normally insisted on three signatures and so, remained, predominantly a bankers' bank. It always maintained a very large reserve. The law of 1803 placed France on a bimetallic standard, and the bank commonly cashed its notes in silver. After 1875, however, gold was the only metal suitable for export, and the bank strove to build up its gold reserve, which, by 1907, accounted for about four-fifths of total reserves.

The only other banking development before 1848 was the foundation of a large number of small banks doing discount and deposit business. These banks remained numerous throughout the century, but their importance declined greatly in face of competition from the big joint-stock banks. The first of these, the Comptoir National d'Escompte de Paris, was founded as an emergency measure in 1848 and was followed by the Credit Industriel et Commercial (1859), the Credit Lyonnais (1863) and the Societe Generale de Credit (1864). These banks set out to develop the check system and attracted deposits by opening a nation-wide network of branches and offering attractive rates of interest. They participated to some extent in the issue of

44

industrial shares, but their advances to industry were very limited; by far the most important part of their business with industry and commerce was in the form of discounts.

A few institutions on the periphery of the banking world deserve mention, The Credit Foncier and the Credit Mobilier were both formed in 1852; both did a limited deposit business, but the former was chiefly an agricultural mortgage company and the latter an investment bank. The Credit Mobilier after a spectacular career, was liquidated in 1867, but   the   Credit   Foncier remained an important part of the French financial system. The successors of the Credit Mobilier were the banques d'afaires, of which the first was the Banque de Paris et des Pays Bas (1872); these firms were chiefly concerned with the marketing of industrial securities and, although they accepted deposits from firms with which they had dealings, they did not seek them from the general public.

Germany—There were few banks of any significance in Germany, before the middle of the 19th century. The Bank of Prussia, forerunner of the Reichsbank, did only a small and old-
fashioned business until 1846, when it received a new constitution and began to grow rapidly. The old Hamburg Giro bank continued its business until absorbed by the Reichsbank in 1875. The Seehandlung, formed as a state-owned trading company by Frederick the Great, acted as banker to the Prussian government and did a limited general business. There were wealthy, merchant bankers engaged in international finance, and the Rothschilds were extending their
activities from Frankfurt over the whole of Europe; but the local private banker was still doing only a small and primitive business. Banks of issue were subject to regulation by the various states; the first was formed in Bavaria in 1834, and there were 33 in existence in 1875.

The Bank of Prussia was transformed into the Reichsbank in 1875. The capital was privately owned, but the representatives of the shareholders had mainly advisory functions; the bank was managed, by a president, vice-president and directorate appointed by the Emperor on the
nomination of the bundesrat and was subject to the supervision of a state-appointed curatorium. The act of 1875 regulated the issue bank notes. Each bank received an "indirect contingent" of notes not covered by cash (the Reichsbank received 250,000,000 marks out of   a   total   of 360,000,000), and there was a tax of 5% on uncovered issues in excess of this. It was further provided that all notes must be covered by a reserve of one-third in gold, current coin   or imperial notes (an issue fixed in 1874 at 120,000,000 marks). By 1905 only four banks besides the Reichsbank retained their issues, and these accounted for only 6% of the total bank-note circulation. Reichsbank notes, were made legal tender in 1909.

The Reichsbank was required to provide banking facilities for the whole empire, and no other central bank used the <u>branch system</u> so extensively. Within 30 years from its foundation the bank established about 100 main branches and more than 4,000 sub offices. With the development of the branches went that of the transfer system. Even persons without an account might, for a small fee, pay money in for transfer to anyone holding an account anywhere in Germany and this service was very widely used. The Reichsbank was obliged by its charter to act as banker to the empire and the states free of charge. Most of its private lending was by way of discount. The official rate was usually higher than that of the other banks but in 1880 the Reichsbank began to make discounts at a lower "private" rate in times of <u>easy money;</u> it handled a much larger proportion of the total discount business of the country than did most central banks. The bank, like the Bank of England, was obliged to buy gold at fixed minimum price and to pay its notes in gold; and it acted from the first as keeper of the central gold reserve and lender of last resort. These obligations of a central bank imply a general regulation of credit; and the chief instrument for this was discount policy, involving both variations in the official rate and in the bank's readiness to discount at the "private" rate. At times the bank also tried to protect its reserve by making interest-free advances to importers of gold and by buying gold at more than the statutory price.

The main differences in the business of the English and German joint-stock banks were the lower cash ratio and larger bill holdings of the German banks and their closer association with industry. Contrary, to a widely held opinion, the German banks did not deliberately hold long-term industrial stock; but they did take, a very big part in the issue of such stock and, when an issue miscarried, might be left with substantial holdings which they, would have to retain for some time. The banks were frequently represented on the boards of firms which they assisted in this way, and their control over industry was increased by the widespread practice of voting stock deposited with them by customers. The banks were also most energetic in forming subsidiaries and establishing agencies abroad, and their activities in this way were conspicuous in Italy, Romania and Bulgaria, in the near and far east and in South America.

Other European Countries—The other counties of Europe showed wide variety in their banking systems. In general, those of northwestern Europe were the most mature; those of southeastern Europe, the least. In most countries savings banks and mortgage companies were important parts of the financial system, and in the Austrian empire, Italy and Poland it is difficult to, draw a line between them and the commercial banks. The commercial banks of Scandinavia and the Netherlands tended to confine themselves to deposit banking on the English model; those of Austria, Italy, Switzerland and, to a lesser extent, Belgium followed the German pattern in associating closely with industry; and those of eastern Europe were chiefly concerned with agricultural finance. All the major countries set up central banks, sometimes in private hands, sometimes with state participation; in some there was no special commercial banking legislation, while in others the powers and working of the banks were carefully regulated. The oldest joint-stock commercial bank in Europe, the Societe General pour favoriser l'Industrie Nationale (later Societe Generale de Belgique) of Belgium, was founded in 1822. In 1850 the National Bank of Belgium was formed, taking over the note issues of the older joint stock banks and acting as fiscal agent for the state. Other banks were formed during the second half of the 19th century, and by 1913 there were 70 of them, but the Societe Generale was by far the most important. In the Netherlands the Bank of the Netherlands was founded in 1814. There was a flourishing private banking system; but joint-stock banking did ,not begin until after 1860, and growth was comparatively slow.

In Scandinavia the Bank of Sweden (oldest surviving bank in the world at mid-20th century) dates from 1668, but Swedish private banking did not begin until about 1830 and joint-stock commercial banking until 1864. Joint-stock banks were not allowed to issue notes, but private banks could do so until 1897, when all issues were centralized with the Bank of Sweden. There¬ after no new private banks were formed; altogether there were about 80 banks in 1913. The system in Finland closely resembled that of Sweden, private banking beginning in the 1860s and joint-stock banking in the 1880s. The first Norwegian bank, other than the Bank of Norway, (1814). was not founded until 1848; thereafter progress was gradual, and the system remained highly decentralized with many small local banks. In Denmark joint-stock banking began in 1846, and there were no less than 144 banks in 1913, though 7 of them accounted for two-thirds of total deposits.

The Austro-Hungarian system comprised three parts, centered on Vienna, Budapest and Prague, of which the last was the least important. The Austrian section was dominated, in 1913, by ten big Viennese banks, which had grown up on the German model with extraordinarily close relations with industry and trade, while in Hungary there were a few large and very many small banks concerned largely with agricultural finance.

Switzerland had a tradition of private banking, and Swiss joint-stock banking began with the local "discount banks" formed ,between 1820 and 1840. Several bigger banks were founded after 1860 to finance railway and industrial development, and these grew into the most important element in the system. The cantonal banks were formed in the third quarter of the 19th century primarily to assist agriculture, but some also did a general banking business. The central bank,' the Swiss National bank, was not founded until 1905.

In Italy a number of note-issuing banks were formed in the separate states during the 1840s, and there was a rapid development of the banks closely associated with industry after the unification of the country. The National Bank of the Sardinian States, formed in 1849 by merging two banks of Genoa (1844) and Turin (1847), became the National Bank of the Kingdom of Italy. A crisis in 1893 provided the opportunity for a syndicate headed by the Discontogesellschaft and other big German banks to form the Banca Commerciale Italiana (1894), which grew into one of the most important banks in the country. In 1913 five large banks controlled two-thirds of all deposits; of these the Credito Italiano as well as the Banca Commerciale had some German participation.

Modern Spanish banking began with the formation of the Bank of St. Charles in 1782. In 1844 the Bank of Isabella U was formed; and in 1847 the two banks merged. In 1856 the combined bank was reorganized as the Bank of Spain with a monopoly of banking activity throughout the country. The bank issued notes, operated current accounts and, did some discount business but was heavily involved in the unsatisfactory Spanish state finances and was in difficulties throughout the century.

Banking in Russia dates from 1768. when Catherine U set up two banks of issue in Moscow. The Russian State bank was founded in 1860, and the first joint-stock commercial bank in 1865. The banking system was not, however, highly developed and depended considerably on French and German capital. The immature banking systems of other eastern European countries also relied largely on foreign capital, German in Romania and Bulgaria, French and British in Greece.

The 20th Century—World War I brought a general increase in bank deposits and involved most banks in large purchases of government securities. Its aftermath included great territorial and political changes in many counties and currency disturbances in almost all. The period 1919-29 was mainly occupied with these problems. Central banks were set up in the new countries (Poland, Czechoslovakia, Hungary, Yugoslavia, Estonia, Latvia and Lithuania); and the Bank of Spain was reorganized as a true central bank in 1921. The new countries all endeavored to build national banking systems. In the former Austro-Hungarian empire, the Hungarian system, grew up from the big Budapest banks. A central corporation of banking companies was formed in 1916 and remained after the war, with powers of inspection over member banks. Branches of Austrian banks in Czechoslovakia were either liquidated, taken over by Prague banks or formed into new Czech companies, while Yugoslavia made some progress in building a national system on. the much more primitive foundations existing there. The sphere of influence of the Austrian banks was thus greatly restricted, and there were several amalgamations, as a result of which, the big Viennese banks were reduced to four by 1929. In former Russian Poland there had been eight Polish commercial banks and three state institutions doing some banking business. These continued after liberation and a number of new banks were formed.

The timing of inflation and deflation varied considerably between countries. In the inflationary period new banks were formed and the nominal though not the real value of deposits increased, while deflation and stabilization brought liquidations and further concentration in banking systems. Deflation was first felt in Scandinavia in 1921; both in Norway and Sweden the state gave emergency assistance, and there were a large number of closures. In France, Belgium and the Netherlands there was less change in banking structure, but some concentration took place in France through the big banks' extending their branches and, in Belgium and the Netherlands, gaining control of smaller provincial banks. The German system underwent great change. In 1924 the Reichsbank was reconstituted under a general council (half of which was foreign), with its discount policy restricted and without the power to buy long-term securities. A subsidiary, the Gold Discount Bank, was established to assist foreign trade and was later used for a wide variety of purposes. The big commercial bank suffered heavy losses in the inflation and had to face competition from new banks formed for particular industrial groups and from public institutions (one of which, the Reichskreditgesellschaft, formed in 1922, was a full-fledged commercial bank). A series of amalgamations between 1914 and 1929 reduced the big Berlin banks from nine to five. In Italy the Banco di Sconto was in difficulties in 1921 and was replaced by the Banca Nazionale di Credito, which amalgamated (merged) with the Credito Italiano in 1930. A comprehensive banking law of 1926 provided for registration of all banks, state approval for all new banks or branches and inspection by the Bank of Italy; and in 1930 all note issues were placed in the hands of the Bank of Italy.

The great depression which began at the end of 1929 hit the banks of many counties. The failure of the Austrian Credit-Anstalt in May 1931 had repercussions throughout central Europe, and before the depression was ended the state had to take special measures in Austria, Germany, Hungary, Czechoslovakia, Sweden, Italy and Belgium. The German crisis was the most acute: the Deutsche, Commerz-, Dresdner and Darmstadter banks were all assisted by the state; the two last were amalgamated, and at one time the Gold Discount bank held 90% of the capital of the combined bank. Later, however, the special advances were repaid and the capital returned to private hands. The crisis was followed by legal changes affecting both central and commercial banks. Central banks were given more freedom of action in Austria, Poland, Czechoslovakia, Sweden, Hungary; Denmark and Yugoslavia by reducing the amount, of reserve required by law and in Germany, France, Poland, the Netherlands, Hungary and Lithuania by extending their powers in respect of open-market dealings. The constitution of the Reichsbank was changed in 1933, when the general council was abolished and the appointment of the president placed in the hands of the, chancellor. In 1936 the Bank of Denmark was nationalized and the Bank of Italy was reorganized.

World War II produced new inflationary pressures everywhere, besides leading to great territorial and political changes. The German banks had penetrated deeply into the financial systems of the occupied countries, but the Allies declared all share purchases by Germans to be void, and foreign affiliates of German banks were liquidated. Currency reform was necessary in many countries after the war. Belgium, Yugoslavia, Denmark, France, the Netherlands,
Czechoslovakia, Austria and Finland made new note issues, and in some of those countries part of the holding of old notes was placed in blocked bank accounts. In the U.S.S.R.,   at   the beginning, of 1948. old rubles were exchanged for new at the rate of one new for ten old, and bank deposits and the value of government bonds were also scaled down, while the German currency reform of June 1948 also involved drastic cancellations of the old currency.

The banking systems of Estonia. Latvia and Lithuania were incorporated with that of the U.S.S.R. when those states lost their independence; and those of. the countries which passed under Communist control (Poland, Hungary, Czechoslovakia, Bulgaria, Romania and
Yugoslavia) were nationalized. In eastern Germany the old banks were abolished and a new system, resembling that of the U.S.S.R., was created. In the western zones the three large commercial banks (Deutsche, Dresdner and Commerz-) were divided in 1945-46 into 30 small units, each of which was allowed to operate in only one of the II Lander. New .central banks were set up for each state and, as part of the currency reform, there was created the Bank of the German States (Bank Deutscher Lander) at Frankfurt with a monopoly of note issue and limited powers over the state central banks, The 30 commercial banks created in 1945-46 proved too small for efficient operation and, in 1952, the law was amended. The country was divided into three banking regions and the banks   consolidated   into   nine   new   firms,   each   of   which   could operate throughout the whole of one region. To prevent any further concentration, interlocking shareholdings and directorates were prohibited. The central banks of Norway and   the Netherlands were nationalized and that of Belgium was brought under state control. In France the nationalization movement went much further; the law of Dec. 1945 nationalized the bank of France and the four largest commercial banks; in 1946 the two, principal banques d'afaires were nationalized; and the smaller banks, of both kinds, were brought under stringent control.

The war in Korea in 1950 aggravated the inflation which had been a chronic feature of the European economy since World War II, and caused most western European counties to abandon the low and stable interest rates which had survived from the 1930s and I adopt more "orthodox" monetary policies. There was a general rise in interest rates in 1950-51 and,

thereafter, central banks varied their rates according to the economic circumstances of their respective countries. In most cases the new policy involved only the more active use of powers already possessed by central banks, but in some counties (e.g. the Netherlands in 1954) central banking powers were substantially increased..

B. GREAT BRITAIN AND THE COMMONWEALTH

England—Medieval English finance was less developed than that of the great continental centers, and much of it was in the hands of aliens. Financiers were mainly concerned with loans to the crown, with the collection and transmission of papal revenues and with the finance of foreign trade. They used money deposited with them as well as their own capital. Bills of exchange were widely used but did not yet circulate as money, and bank notes unknown. The type of loan which might be made was severely restricted by the usury laws. The Reformation brought a change of ideas on this subject, and from 1545 the state merely fixed a maximum rate of interest. The Tudor period was one of expanding trade, capital accumulation and increasing opportunities for financial transactions. Merchants like Sir Thomas Gresham played a growing pat in the finance of foreign trade, and the London scriveners began to lend money, both their own and that which they had borrowed for the purpose.

The direct ancestors of modern banks were, however, neither the merchants nor the scriveners but the goldsmiths. At first the goldsmiths accepted deposits merely for safekeeping; but early in the 17th century their deposit receipts were circulating in place of money itself and so became the first English bank notes. Soon the goldsmiths began to issue notes not only against the deposit of coin but also by way of loan, and this was the beginning of fractional-reserve banking in England. The goldsmiths flourished during the Great Rebellion, but some of them lost heavily on their loans to Charles II; some went bankrupt but others, such as Child's and Hoare's, survived and grew to be leaders among the London private banks of the 18th and 19th centuries.

The 18th Century—The financial difficulties of the crown continued after the revolution of 1689, and led, in 1694, to the foundation of the Bank of England (q.v.). The bank lent £1,200,000 to the government (later followed by other loans) in return for a charter of incorporation and, in 1697, was granted a monopoly of joint-stock banking in England and Wales. In 1707 it became the principal agent for the circulation of exchequer bills and in 1715 it acted, for the first time, as agent for the issue and management of a government loan.
Gradually, during the next 40 years, it became banker to the exchequer and the principal government departments, holding their deposits and paying their drafts as any bank does for its customers.

The Bank of England also did ordinary banking business, issuing notes, receiving deposits and discounting bills of exchange. But its role as banker to the state and its monopoly of joint-stock banking placed it in a unique position; and in its relations with the private banks it soon became much more than just a privileged competitor about. 1770 the London private bankers (survivors of the old gold smith bankers reinforced by a number of new firms) practically ceased to issue their own notes and used Bank of England notes instead. Most of them opened drawing accounts with the Bank of England, as also did the Royal Bank of Scotland. The country banks

managed their business in the capital through a correspondent, generally one of the private bankers. The Bank of England's reserve of gold could thus be drawn upon in time of crisis by these London banks and, through them, by all the multitude of small banks which were springing up all over England in the second half of the 18th century. To meet this obligation the Bank of England had to accumulate a large reserve, and most of the country's gold stock not in actual circulation came to be concentrated in its vaults.

Thus by the end of the 18th century the Bank of England was performing, though not yet fully, several of the recognized functions of a central bank; it acted as banker to the government,
manager of the public debt, bankers' bank and custodian of most of the country's gold reserve. It did not yet, however, recognize the responsibility of acting as "lender of last resort" or accept the supreme duty of a central bank; viz., that of exercising a general direction and control over monetary affairs.

Cash reserves, which varied greatly in size, were held partly in gold but chiefly in Bank of England notes. The more prudent bankers invested some of their assets in government securities, and loans were made on mortgage-to farmers on the security of stock; to businessmen often on personal security only. The most-important and general means of lending was, however, by the discounting of bills of exchange; banks in country districts often had
difficulty in getting as many bills as they wanted whereas those in expanding manufacturing areas were under constant pressure for loans and therefore began to sell bills to those in agriculture¬ districts through agents in London, who thus constituted, in the early 19th century, the origin of the London discount market.

Central Banking. 1793-1844—The wars with France of 1793-1815 imposed a great strain on the English monetary system, and in 1797 the government, by order in council, forbade the Bank of England to pay its notes in gold, which restriction was confirmed by parliament and continued in force until 1821. Freed from the necessity of cash payment, both the Bank of England and the country banks thereupon increased the amount of their note issues and the volume of their lending; the government continued its inflationary methods of war finance; prices rose; the foreign-exchange rates fell; and gold bullion was sold in the market at a
premium over its mint price.

These events led to much controversy and to a parliamentary inquiry which produced the famous Bullion report (Report of the Select Committee on the High Price of Gold Bullion, 1810). The policy of the Bank of England's directors was to meet what they called "the legitimate needs of commerce" by discounting all good bills brought to them at a rate of 5%, the maximum allowed by the usury laws; they maintained that the resulting increase in their note issue had no influence upon prices or the foreign exchanges. The directors' critics,

including such great economists as David Ricardo, Thomas Robert Malthus and Henry Thornton, though they disagreed over details, all maintained that there was a close connection between the volume of Bank of England notes and the level of prices and further that the level of prices affected the foreign-exchange rates and thus the inflow or outflow of gold and the reserve of the bank. Once this chain of reasoning was accepted it followed that the bank, as custodian of the central gold reserve of the country, must shape its lending policy according to general economic conditions and so as to exercise a general control over money and credit. This critical period was thus of the highest importance in the development of central banking theory.

Only four years after the resumption of cash payments there occurred, in 1825. one of the most violent financial crises of the century. The course of events was one which became familiar, with slight variations, in later years; a rise in domestic prices and the value of imports caused the exchanges to fall and the Bank of England's reserve to be depleted; then a few big business failures precipitated a run on the banks and a further drain on the reserve, not for export but for domestic circulation. The remedy, which became classical, was for the bank to raise its discount rate to protect its reserve against the foreign drain and then to lend freely at the high rate in order to maintain confidence at home (the function of "lender of last resort"). In 1825 the bank allowed its reserve to fall dangerously low before taking protective action; nevertheless, at the height of the panic, it discounted all eligible bills and even relaxed its rules of eligibility.

The act renewing the bank's charter, in 1833 made, three more important changes in the law: (1) Bank of England notes were made legal tender; (2) the usury laws were repealed as far as they affected bills of exchange, setting the bank free to raise its discount rate above 5% and paving the way for the use of variations in bank rate as an instrument of policy; and (3) joint stock banks were declared to be legal even within the limit of 65 mi. provided that they did not issue notes. Public dissatisfaction with the Bank of England was aggravated by father crises in 1836 and 1839, and criticism developed into a controversy between what are usually known as the Currency school and the Banking school. The Currency school, led by Samuel Jones Lloyd (Baron Overstone), Robert Torrens and George Warde Norman, laid great stress on the close connection between the amount of money and prices; they denied money as gold and bank notes and from that deduced their main proposition, that the total of notes and coin in circulation ought to be made to vary in exactly the same way as would a purely metallic currency. The Banking school, led by Thomas Tooke and John Fullarton. pointed out the importance of other instruments of credit and argued that a varying amount of credit could be built up on a given cash base; they were no less critical of the policy of the bank than their opponents but did not wish to see it fettered by any rigid legal restrictions.

The Bank Charter act of 1844 embodied the views of the Currency school. The bank was divided into an issue department and a banking department. It was allowed a fiduciary issue (backed by government securities) of £14,000,000, (£ = pound) beyond which amount all notes had to be covered by gold or silver (the silver not to exceed one-fifth of the whole); and was obliged to buy gold at £3 17s. 9d. a standard ounce and to pay its notes in gold coin, which was equivalent to selling gold at £3 17s. 10 1/2d. an ounce. The note issue served both for the use of the public and as a reserve for the banking department. No new banks of issue were to be allowed; existing ones were limited to their average circulation in the three months prior to the introduction of the bill; and any bank which ceased to issue, stopped payment or amalgamated (merged) so as to give itself more than six partners was to forfeit its rights, whereupon the Bank of England was authorized to raise its own fiduciary issue by two-thirds of the permitted issue of the forfeiting bank. The last country bank to issue notes did not cease until 1921, but country banks' issues had become insignificant long before this.

Developments. 1844-1914.—The first provincial joint-stock banks were formed at Huddersield and Bradford in 1827. The act of 1833 was followed the next year by the foundation   of   the London and Westminster bank, with a great banker, J. W. Gilbat, as manager. Gilbart had to fight both the Bank of England, which refused him a drawing account, and the London private bankers, who refused him admission to their clearinghouse; but his bank prospered and was soon followed by others. By 1841 there were 115 joint-stock banks in England and Wales, and the number of private banks had fallen to 321. After this boom, however, promotion of joint stock banks diminished, and the structure of the system remained fairly stable until the great amalgamations at the end of the century; in 1886 there were 117 joint-stock banks but more than 250 private ones still in existence, the chief change since 1841 having been the extension of the branch system by the joint-stock banks.

The 50 years before 1844 had seen the evolution of central banking theory; the next 50 saw the Bank of England experimenting with its techniques of credit control and gaining steadily in power and experience, although in 1847, 1857 and 1866 it had to obtain from the government permission to exceed its legal issue with the promise of a bill of indemnity if it broke the law. The Bank of England allowed its private business to dwindle and concentrated on   central banking; the commercial banks increased their balances with the Bank of England; and the system was developed whereby those balances were replenished, when necessary, by calling in loans from the discount market, the bill brokers then trying to borrow elsewhere and going to the Bank of England only in the last resort.

The main methods of credit control were bank rate and open-market operations, Bank rate, used experimentally before 1844, was used regularly soon afterward and became more important toward the end of the century, when other banks came to ix their rates for loans and deposits in relation to it. Open-market operations were a means of making bank rate "effective"; i.e., of preventing other shot-term interest rates from falling too far below bank rate.   The   Bank   of England would sell securities, thus taking money out of the market, when it wished to raise -
rates and buy them when it wished to ease credit. After the Baring crisis 1890, in which the Bank of England took the lead in averting a panic by raising a guarantee fund for Barings, there was closer co-operation between it and the other banks. This was made easier by the rapid
spread of amalgamation. The Bank of England could now communicate informal hints on policy to the other banks; and in 1911 a more formal arrangement was reached, whereby the Clearing Bankers committee met once a quarter at the bank.

It was only between 1890 and 1918 that English banking came to consist of a few very large banks operating a nation-wide system of branches. The increasing scale of industry was the main reason for the series of amalgamations which brought this about; a subsidiary reason was the public demand for larger reserves that followed the Baring crisis. By 1914 there were only

16 members of the London clearinghouse, 13 of these being great joint-stock banks, and the small local bank was nearly extinct. The Birmingham and Midland bank (forerunner of the Midland bank) absorbed the Central Bank of London in 1891 and the City bank in 1898 to become the London, City and Midland; and in 1897 E. H. Hoi den, the person most responsible for the subsequent pace of amalgamation, had become manager. In 1896 Barclays bank had

been formed by the fusion of 15 private banks, mostly of Quaker origin. In 1902 the Union of London and Smiths was formed by the combination of a London joint-stock bank (the Union), a London private bank (Smith, Payne and Smith) and a number of north midland banks linked with the private bank by family ties. The climax came during a few months in 1917-18;   the Midland absorbed the London Joint Stock bank; the National Provincial absorbed the Union of London and Smiths; the Westminster absorbed Parr's; and Barclays absorbed the London and Provincial and London and South Western, which had themselves amalgamated less than a year before. This spate of amalgamation gave rise to fears of a "money trust" A treasury committee reporting in 1918 suggested legislation making government   approval   necessary   for   further amalgamations; no such law was passed, but the. banks entered into informal understanding not to arrange further mergers without treasury approval.

History From 1914.—The gold standard was inoperative during - World War I and formally suspended from 1919 to 1925. Gold coin was replaced in ordinary circulation by treasury notes, which circulated concurrently with those of the Bank of England until the issue was transferred to the bank in 1928. From 1925 to 1931 gold bullion was freely obtainable at the bank, though gold coin never came back into use; but in 1931 the gold standard was again abandoned, and in 1939 the bank's gold stock was transferred to the exchange equalization account. Thereafter, though the separation of departments established in 1844 was preserved the   bank   held practically no gold, the note issue being wholly fiduciary with its amount fixed by the treasury. The "cheap money" policy which followed the abandonment of the gold standard caused bank rate to fall into abeyance and led to a relaxation of the central bank's control over credit. Such control as it still had was of a qualitative rather than a quantitative nature and exercised through informal contacts and persuasion. Throughout this period the bank worked   in   close   and increasingly harmonious contact with the government. The Bank of-England act came into force on March 1, 1946. Under nationalization the directors were appointed by the crown; the treasury might issue directions to the bank; and the bank could make recommendations and, if necessary, give directions to the commercial banks; The act might seem only to have given formal expression to a relationship that had grown up, by mutual consent, between the three parties; but any government so inclined could use the wide and rather vague powers of direction conferred by it to exercise a much more stringent control over the commercial banks than was at first attempted.

The Labor government, elected in 1945, intensified the drive for cheap money in an effort to bring the yield of long-term government bonds down to 21/2"%. Bank rate was retained at 2%; the Bank of England kept the commercial banks liberally supplied with cash, and there was a rapid growth of deposits. This policy was modified in 1947 and drastically changed, with   a
change of government, in 1951. Bank rate was raised to 2 1/2% in Nov. 1951 and to 4% in March 1952, and the liquidity of the banking system was reduced by the funding of £1,000,000,000 of treasury bills. Thereafter the Bank of England, like the central banks of most other European countries, adopted a flexible policy, reducing bank rate in 1953-54 and raising it again to counteract inflation and a loss of gold reserves in 1955-56, During this period there were a number of technical changes designed to restore to the Bank of England the control over the financial system which it had largely abandoned between 1931 and 1951.

Scotland and Ireland.—Scotland differed from England in having no law against the formation of joint-stock banks and in the early development of branch banking. The core of. the system was constituted by the three chartered banks, the Bank of Scotland (1695), the Royal Bank of Scotland (1727) and the British Linen company (1744). These firms began to found branches in the middle of the 18th century and were joined later by a number of unchartered joint-stock banks. By 1826 there were 36 banks in Scotland, all the most important being joint stock. In 1845 Sir Robert Peel's government followed up the Bank Charter act by regulating Scottish note issues—no new note-issuing banks were to be allowed; and the 19 issuing banks in existence were restricted to a fixed fiduciary issue, further issues to be covered wholly by gold or silver. The privilege of note issue was more significant in Scotland than in England, and no important banks were founded after 1845. Concentration proceeded gradually, and the number of banks was reduced to eight in 1914. Toward the end of the 19th century connections with England grew closer; and in the final stages of the amalgamation movement Barclays acquired control of the British Linen bank; Lloyds, of the National Bank of Scotland; and the Midland, of the Clydesdale bank and the North of Scotland bank (amalgamated in 1949). The Royal Bank of Scotland, however, gained control of Glyn, Mills and Company and of Williams Deacon's. Contrary to the practice in English amalgamations, however, the Scottish banks retained their separate identities.

In Ireland there were many small and weak private banks and a few good ones founded during the 18th century. Of these the most important, was David La Touche and Son, founded by a Huguenot poplin manufacturer around 1700. In 1783 the Bank of Ireland was' chartered with a David La Touche as its first governor; the charter was closely modeled on the Bank of England's. The Bank of Ireland originally had a monopoly of joint-stock banking, but this was modified in 1821 and finally abolished in 1845. The bank acted as government banker and manager of the national debt in Ireland and later as banker and lender of last resort to the Irish commercial banks, but never attained the full stature of a central bank since it relied in time of strain upon the Bank of England, which was the ultimate holder of cash reserves for both countries. Also, the Bank of Ireland, unlike the Bank of England, continued to play an important part in ordinary commercial banking. After 1821 a number of joint-stock banks were formed; and these in 1845 were given their own fiduciary note issues as in Scotland. In the second half of the 19th century the remaining private banks were absorbed by the joint-stock banks, and in 1914 there were nine such banks operating more than 800 branches. One of them, the National, was also a member of the London clearinghouse. As in Scotland, there was some fusion with English banks, the Midland gaining control of the Belfast Banking company, the Westminster of the Ulster bank. The formation of the Irish Free State was followed by the issue of Irish notes under the control of a currency commission (1927) and the establishment of the Central Bank of Ireland (1942), but it did little to disturb the close banking connection between Great Britain and Ireland.

Commonwealth of Nations.—Banks were established in the countries which now form the

British Commonwealth at an early stage in their development. Control over banking varied with the degree of independence attained by the new settlements; initially it was exercised from
London, then by the various state and provincial legislatures, finally by the dominion governments. Private Banks played little part in this field and all the important banks were

joint-stock companies. They naturally had close connections with London, kept reserves in London and formed an important element in the London money market. None of the dominions had a central bank until after World War 1.

Canada.—The banks doing ordinary commercial business in Canada are the chartered banks; the oldest is the Bank of Montreal, founded in 1817 and chartered in 1822. Until 1867 charters were issued by the provinces of Upper Canada and Quebec; subsequently, the regulation of banking was in the hands of the federal government, which granted charters under a series of decennial banking acts, beginning in 1871. Law regulated banking in much more detail in Canada than in most other counties.

There were 28 Canadian chartered banks in 1867 and 20 more were formed between 1867 and 1881; but the number was reduced by amalgamations to 10 in 1931. Branch banking developed early and by 1931 there were more than 3,000 branches. The chartered banks issued their own notes, which formed the main currency of the country until displaced by those of the Bank of Canada after 1934. They also did all ordinary banking business and participated, unlike the English joint-stock banks, in the making of long-term capital issues for industry. The Canadian central bank, the Bank of Canada, was set up by an act of 1934. It acts as banker to the government and to the chartered banks, which were bound to keep a reserve of 5% of their liabilities with it. The Bank of Canada gradually took over the note issue of the chartered banks and also their gold reserves and those of the central note reserve; it is required to keep a gold reserve of 25% of its notes and deposits. In the decennial revisions of the banking law of 1944 and 1954, the banks were allowed to make mortgage loans, and in 1954 the Bank of Canada was empowered to vary the commercial banks' cash ratio. In 1944 the Industrial Development bank was set up to provide long-term finance for industry, and in 1954 the first steps were taken toward the building up of a call-loan market.

Australia.—In Australia the pioneer undertaking was the Bank of New South Wales, founded in 1817 and followed during the next 25 years by 18 other banks. These banks, unlike those of Canada, made loans on land and played a big part in the building-up of the large "squatter" estates. The discovery of gold in 1851 led to a, further boom in bank formations; and when the search for gold subsided, the banks began to play an increasing part in the finance of secondary industry. Connections with England were very close and many banks drew a large part both of capital and of deposits from London at this time. In 1893 a severe financial crisis left some banks with liabilities which they took several years to discharge. Altogether more than 50 banks were formed in the 19th century, but the number was reduced by failures and amalgamations to 16, of which 3 have their head offices and the great part of their shares in England. Up to 1910 the banks had issued their own notes, but in that year a treasury-note issue was established and a penal tax imposed on bank notes. The Commonwealth Bank of Australia, formed in 1911, held the federal account land the accounts of some of the states and was intended to compete with the ordinary trading banks. By acts of 1920 and 1924 the note issue was transferred to it and, especially after 1929, it came to operate more and more as a central bank.

The Bank act of 1945 added to the central banking powers of the Commonwealth bank in several ways, including giving it the right of requiring commercial banks to deposit a variable

amount of their assets in special accounts with it. At the same time the act provided that, in case of difference of opinion between the Commonwealth bank and the government, the federal
treasurer might issue directions to the bank. This power was somewhat modified in 1950 by the setting up of a bank board with half its members drawn from circles outside both the
Commonwealth bank and the government. The 1945 act also created a new industrial finance department of the bank, and encouraged it to develop its ordinary banking business,   so   that
Australia is one of the few countries in which the central bank and the commercial banks are in active competition with one another.

India Pakistan and Ceylon.—In India a banking system of the European type was superimposed upon an indigenous banking system of great antiquity. Besides small local bankers and money¬ lenders there are the joint-stock banks, the Imperial Bank of India, the exchange banks and the Reserve Bank of India. The first joint-stock bank, the Bank of Hindustan, was founded as early as 1770; development was slow during the 19th century but more rapid after 1900, and there was never the process of concentration which took place in Britain and the other countries of the commonwealth. In 1940 there were 180 banks, operating   nearly   1,200   branches,   The
exchange banks, of which the oldest is the Chartered Bank of India, Australia and China, are mainly concerned with international transactions. The Imperial bank was formed in 1921 by the merger of the three presidency banks (Bengal, 1808, Bombay, 1840, and Madras, 1843). The presidency banks had originally possessed the right of note issue, but this was taken over by the government in 1862. The Imperial bank held government balances and acted as a clearinghouse, but never as a true central bank. The Reserve Bank of India was created as a central bank by an act of 1934 and commenced operations in 1935, taking over the note issue   from   the
government.

The creation of the republic of India and of the new dominions of Pakistan and Ceylon led to further changes. In 1948 the State Bank of Pakistan was established as a central bank, with the state owning a controlling interest in its capital. On Jan. 1, 1949, the Reserve Bank of India was nationalized and given increased powers over the commercial banks. In 1954 the   Industrial
Credit and Finance Corporation of India was formed with the co-operation of the International Bank for Reconstruction and Development. In the following year the Indian government took over the Imperial bank with the intention of merging it with a number of small local banks to form a state bank with a nation-wide branch net-work. Pakistan set up a new central bank in 1948, and Ceylon in 1950.

C. HISTORY OF BANKING IN THE UNITED STATES

Banking in the United States had its origins, apart from its rudimentary beginnings in certain colonial institutions, with the grant of a charter (1781) to the Bank of North America. Doubts concerning the legal power of the Continental Congress to grant a charter to a banking institution led the bank successfully to seek a charter from the state of Pennsylvania (1782). The establishment of the Bank of North America was a response to the needs of the Continental Congress, associated with the financing of the American Revolution. In this respect, as in others, the bank was a very successful institution. It made substantial loans to the government, provided credit facilities for private business and issued a currency redeemable in species on demand. The bank's success (it continued under renewed chatters from the state of

57

Pennsylvania until 1864 when it became a national bank, see below) provided encouragement to others. The Bank of Massachusetts was chartered in 1784 and the Bank of New York in 1791. These early institutions were the forerunners of a large number of state banks. One estimate indicates that there were 28 such banks by 1800 and 88 by 1811. This development, implying as it did the need for credit institutions, established the precedent for the far-ranging state banking systems which, apart from the first and second Bank of the United States, constituted the whole of the banking system of the nation until the establishment of the national banks pursuant to the National Bank act of 1863 as amended.

First Bank of the United States (1791-1811).—Establishment of a "national bank" to be the creature and the agency of the national government newly organized ,under the federal constitution was one of the important measures urged by Alexander Hamilton (q.v.), first secretary of the treasury, in developing the powers of the new government. The proposal aroused an important and lasting controversy, for it directly involved certain basic issues upon which Jeffersonian and Hamiltonian principles were to remain divided, There was opposition not only on the general ground that a banking monopoly was incompatible with U.S. ideals, but also on the particular ground that the federal congress had no authority under the constitution to issue corporate charters. The Federalist majority in congress followed Hamilton's proposal; and a charter was enacted. The bank began business in 1791, with a capital of $10,000,000, of which the government owned one-fifth and was the largest stockholder. The bank's charter ran for 20 years, but political opposition and the ineffective organization of the bank's supporters prevented its renewal.

Experience meanwhile had developed a function for the bank that had not been foreseen, viz., its regulation of the private banks. At this time note issue continued to be a more important or at least a more conspicuous, feature of banking than were deposits, and bank notes, which entered circulation as the money that banks went to their borrowers, comprised much the greater part of the total amount of currency in circulation. Since the country was growing fast, there was a powerful and hopeful demand for loans which tended to produce an overextension of credit. Consequently it was to the general interest that expansion be restrained from proceeding to extremes from which recovery was bound to be costly and painful. The Bank of the United States imposed such restraint automatically. As depository of the government, with offices in the' chief seaports and commercial centers, it constantly received from collectors of revenue the notes of private banks with which dues to the government were paid. As fast as it received these notes, it called for their redemption in gold and silver by the banks of issue, automatically restricting thereby the overextension of credit and protecting the economy from <u>inflation</u>. Conversely, in periods of panic and deflation, the bank could ease the pressure.

Essentially, it was engaged in what was subsequently called central banking. The first Bank of the United States was successful as a banking institution. Political opposition supported by those who objected to the restraints with which the growing number of state banks were faced as a consequence of the bank's practice of presenting state bank notes for redemption led to the lapse of its charter. The officers of the bank successfully sought a state charter in New York and continued to operate as a state bank.

Second Bank of the United States (1816-36).—Shortly after discontinuance of the first Bank of the United States, economic conditions made it evident that re-establishment was necessary, and congress in 1816 chartered a new institution with wider powers than before and with closer links to the government. Although the new bank made a good start, it was for a time grossly mismanaged, and did not really prosper until after 1823, when "Nicholas Biddle"   (q.v.)   of Philadelphia became its president. Under Biddle its central banking responsibilities seem to have been as consciously recognized and developed as were those of the Bank of England at the same time—perhaps more so. But since these responsibilities had usually to be exercised as restraints, private banks resented them and complained of oppression. It was a period when
developments in industry and transportation were enhancing the richness of U.S. resources, and when the idea of democracy was beginning to connote free enterprise and laissez-faire. Hence the very conditions that made restraint upon credit advisable made it objectionable.

This opposition to the Bank of the United States on the part of the more speculative and impatient men of business united incongruously with the traditional agrarian opposition to it. The agrarians disliked all banks, associating them with privilege, wealth and aristocracy; and they disliked the Bank of the United States because it was the biggest and because it was a creature of the federal government, the growth of which they had always feared. Opposition to the bank centered behind the leadership of Andrew Jackson (q.v.), who had become president in 1829; his attack and the bank's unsuccessful defense are matters of political history, the bank war being one of the most bitterly contraveded episodes in U.S. history. Again   the constitutional issue was raised; nor did a leading decision of the U.S. supreme court (McCulloch v. Maryland, 1819) upholding the constitutionality of the bank prevent the constant reiteration of this theme. Again, too, it was alleged that the bank was a monopoly antithetical to the ideals of the U.S. Clearly the restraining influence which the bank exercised resulted in the pressures which led President Jackson to prevent the renewal of its charter. In 1832 congress renewed the bank's charter, which was to, expire in 1836; Jackson vetoed the act and, arranged to have the government's funds deposited in banks incorporated under state law. Practically speaking, this cut the bank's operating contact with the government and ended its performance of the central banking function.

During the period of the bank war and of Jackson's second term, 1833-37, economic activity was intense, prices were rising and speculation was feverish. The bank made some attempt at to restrain, but its effectiveness was gone. Moreover, in expectation that it would not continue, there was a general move to set up new local banks. In May 1837 the boom burst   with   a disastrous flood of bankruptcies and slackening of business, and all the banks of the country stopped paying out specie (money). A year later payments were resumed under the leadership of New York bankers, the primacy of New York as the country's financial center being thereby established. There was still a long aftermath of banking trouble, however. In effect, the federal government in ending the Bank of the United States without alternative, abandoned responsibility for the monetary system. The constitution plainly purposed to take all such responsibility from the individual states and lodge it in the federal government, and since bank liabilities in the form of circulating notes constituted the principal part of the Circulating medium, the federal government's responsibility included regulation of bank notes. That responsibility was not resumed until 1863.

The State Banks (1816-63)—The lapse of the charter of the first Bank of the United States in 1811 encouraged the establishment of additional state banks which increased from 88 in 1811 to 246 by 1816. The growth in the number of state banks continued even after the establishment of the second Bank of the United States in 1816, approximating 330 by 1829 and 788 by 1837. It is generally agreed that while the regulations of the several states with respect to banking varied enormously, they were directed—even in the best of circumstances-primarily toward the control of the note liabilities of banks, ignoring essentially the bank's liability to depositors. A large
number of the newly established banks followed banking practices generally thought to be unsound, particularly with respect to note issue and to appropriate provision for the redemption of notes. During this period legislative attitudes in the several states respecting banking ranged from a prohibition thereof to a nearly complete abdication of public responsibility for banking practices. As one might expect, this range of attitudes led to quite sound banking practices in certain areas and to the most serious abuses of financial responsibility in others. In the early years of this period, charters were issued to banks by the several states by special legislative enactment. This practice allegedly, and the evidence in numerous cases bears out the allegation led to corruption and bribery associated with bills to grant corporate charters to banks and, in turn, led to the establishment in many states of "free" banking, a system which provided that banks, like other business enterprises, were to be viewed as "associations," not "corporations." In New York it was provided that notes issued by such "associations" be secured by pledges of state bonds.

The laws of the several states respecting free banking varied greatly and produced both good results and bad. The results in Alabama, Florida, Illinois, Kentucky, Mississippi, Michigan, North Carolina and many other states were very unfavorable, whereas Indiana, Louisiana, Missouri, Ohio and Virginia established sound and successful banking systems each having a central bank with branches. In general, however, and taking the country as a whole   into
account, the banking system, consisting as it did of many separate state systems, was chaotic. This situation, was particularly clear in respect of the issue of bank notes which constituted a much larger part of the circulating medium than is true in the 21st-century (because of the comparative growth of demand deposits); several early efforts at control, both private and public, centered around note issue.

The Suffolk System (1818-58).—This system provides an illustration of private control of bank-note issue by bankers. This system was created by the Suffolk bank of Boston. It was a common thing throughout the country for notes to turn up in cities far from the banks that had issued them, and because of the difficulty and expense of getting such notes redeemed they circulated at a discount. Some brokers and bankers specialized in the collection of notes if they could reduce the expense of collection to less than the discount. The Suffolk bank arranged to redeem the notes of New England banks which would maintain balances with it, and to make the plan effective it systematically called on other banks for payment of their   notes.   The
Suffolk, in fact, paralleled the function of the Bank of the United States and was itself in a rudimentary way engaged in central banking. In one important, respect it was more advanced than the Bank of the United States, for other banks maintained with it balances to which their notes were debited, whereas the Bank of the United States, as it received the notes   of   other

banks, demanded payment accordingly. The Bank of the United States, in other words, regulated banks as their creditor; the Suffolk regulated them as their debtor. The latter relation became typical of modern central banking. Although the Suffolk bank was an efficient
regulator, it was pre-emptory and severe toward other banks, whose hostility had, greatly modified its operations by 1858, shortly before the National Bank act ended state bank-note issue.

A public attempt to the same purpose was represented by the New York Safety fund established by legislative enactment in 1829. The provisions of the act required the maintenance by the banks of a general fund—administered by the state—for the redemption of the notes of banks that failed. This was in a real sense a forerunner of the Federal Deposit Insurance corporation (FDIC). The fund was made proportional to the assets of the several banks instead of to their note issues, which would have been more reasonable. When the fund was held to be, in essence, a guarantee of bank deposits, as well as notes, difficulties which otherwise could have been avoided became insurmountable. New York thereafter adopted, in connection with its free banking policy, provision of law which required that associations freely engaged in banking might issue notes only upon deposit of securities of the United States or of New York with the state comptroller. This method of restraining the note issue and of protecting the note holder was relatively sound and it was the precursor of the method of note issue provided by the
National Bank act of 1863.

The Condition of the Currency to 1863.—Despite the meritorious efforts of the Suffolk bank, of the New York Safety fund and of other reasonably appropriate bases for bank-note issue, it may be said that the condition of the currency in the country as a whole was deplorable, and increasingly so, in the years prior to the Civil War. The state bank notes constituted a most varied currency; varied in design, size and material, and varied, too, in respect of degrees of protection of the note holder and of limitation of total issue. Consequently, apart from the notes of the New York banks and of the New England banks (because of the Suffolk system), most state bank notes had only local circulation. So varied and numerous were the notes issued that at one time, so it is reported, about 1,600 banks issued in all approximately 10,000 different kinds of notes. Every principal financial house made use of a publication known as a "note detector," which purported to identify counterfeit and genuine notes; and the notes of the several state banks circulated, in parts distant from their place of origin (if at all), at discounts ranging up to 10% and 15%. It was this unsatisfactory condition of the currency of the country, together with needs associated with the financing of the Civil War, which led to the passage of the National Bank act in 1863.

National Bank Act of 1863.—In 1863 the federal government resumed its monetary responsibilities with the National Bank act, which provided that banks under federal charter and known as national banks should issue notes on the security of United States government bonds pledged in Washington, D.C., with the comptroller of the currency. These notes were uniform and of standard denomination, and provision for their redemption, modeled after the procedure followed by the Suffolk bank, gave the country a currency that circulated everywhere at par. The immediate incentive to passage of the act was not banking or currency reform, though that was achieved by it, but increased funds for waging the Civil War, the expectation being that national banks would buy great quantities of government bonds in order that they might issue as large a volume of notes as possible. This expectation was disappointed; the deposit business of banks already exceeded their note circulation and was growing far more rapidly. Moreover, the, system was not established till so late in the war that it could not contribute significantly to the financing thereof.

It had been expected also that national charters would be so attractive that state banks would convert to the national system; and when this did not occur, a tax of 10% was imposed on state bank notes, the assumption being that this would render note issue unprofitable and drive state banks out of existence. But this assumption, again, was based on the false notion that note circulation was essential to banking. So state banks that had no circulation remained untouched, and others gave it up, continuing as banks of deposit only. The National Bank act was based in its essentials and in much of its language upon the New York Free Banking act, which had already been the pattern for bank laws in many other states. It provided that any number of banks might be established, the organization of each having to satisfy certain stipulations of the law. It continued and amplified official bank examination, which was to become an increasingly important characteristic of United States banking.

After adoption of the National Bank act the most important monetary and banking measures were those taken by the federal government. Before the Civil War, banking practice and banking control were diverse and experimental. Different states followed different courses— some being restrictive, some being loose, some having a good experience, some having disasters and some changing from one thing to another. Beginning with the National Bank act, banking practice and banking legislation developed a new national unity. Substantial improvements in banking practice resulted there from, particularly with respect to the currency. National bank notes circulated at par throughout the country, the note holder was entirely protected by virtue of the redemption provision and the federal government's liability in the matter was covered through the pledge of U.S. securities with the comptroller of the currency by the issuing banks. The system which emerged under the National Bank act had, however, certain inherent defects which resulted in frequent bank failures and recurrent financial stringency. The defects related both to the factors affecting the volume of currency and to the concentration or "pyramiding" of bank reserves.

The currency, while entirely "safe" as indicated above, failed to expand and contract in volume in response to the changing needs of the business community because through the bond security requirements it was more clearly, related to the fiscal operations of the federal government than it was to the level of economic activity. The national banks were required, to hold reserves in varying proportions to their deposits, depending upon the location of the bank. The banks in the central reserve cities; New York; Chicago and St. Louis, were required to hold their reserves in the form of vault cash; however, the banks in reserve cities (a substantial number of other financial centers) were permitted to hold a proportion of their reserves in the form of deposits with other banks in the central reserve cities, and the so-called country banks (national banks located neither in central reserve nor reserve cities) were permitted to hold a proportion of their reserve in the form of deposits with national banks located in reserve cities of either category. This system produced the pyramiding of reserves noted above, the concentration being most serious in New York. It is widely believed that this concentration led to recurrent financial panics since, in periods of monetary stringency, many banks would call upon their reserve city correspondent banks for cash. This action, in turn, would involve substantial withdrawals from the New York city banks and the latter—being aware of this eventuality—typically had their funds invested in call money loans which would have to be called with consequent liquidation and declines in security prices.

To these substantial defects must be added certain others, some major and some minor: provisions for the clearing of checks were inefficient or unsatisfactory and there was no unified "banking system" in the sense of a central bank with powers to influence and control the flow of money and credit. During this period, moreover, the independent treasury system established in 1836 continued to be operative in spite of the fact that national banks could be employed both as fiscal agents and depositories'. The defects here described led to serious discussions of the monetary and banking system, culminating in the establishment of a national   monetary commission in 1908 and leading, ultimately, to the establishment of the federal reserve system (q.v.). The enactment of the federal reserve system in 1913 effected substantial improvements in the banking system of the United States but—at least in its original formulation—it   fell   far short of meeting the most important requirements of a central banking system.

Bank Suspensions and Crisis of 1933.—Beginning before 1900 there was a prolonged increase in the number of banks, which for the whole country more than doubled between 1900 an 1920. Most of this increase was in farm regions and comprised small banks that could survive only under the most favorable conditions. About 1920 a fall in agricultural prices occurred which immensely reduced the income of farmers and made impossible the situation of those who had gone into debt in the period of prosperity. The upper Mississippi valley states, which were predominantly agricultural, were as a region subjected to a general reduction of income while remaining under the necessity of repaying indebtedness and purchasing supplies. The creditors and suppliers were largely in the eastern industrial regions   so   that   there   arose what is known in international trade as an adverse balance of payments, the agricultural west owing more to the outside world than it received therefrom for the products it sold. The banks were inescapably involved as their deposits dwindled and as their debtors became unable   to pay. Bank failures became common. From 1921 to 1933 the number of banks was reduced by about 16,000—a reduction that offset the corresponding growth of the earlier two decades. It was not all a matter of insolvencies, for many banks consolidated and some liquidated without loss. Most of the contraction occurred among the small banks in the middle west which were, of course, the most vulnerable. Iowa, for example, which in 1924 had 1,600 banks, lost 1,000 of them by 1934.

The great Depression (still the worst in U.S. History) started in 1929. By Jan. 1933 <u>panic began</u> to spread eastward. Holidays, or moratoria, were proclaimed in state after state in order that banks might close under cloak of legality and avoid devastating runs, and almost the first act of the Roosevelt administration, on March 6, 1933, was a proclamation making the closure nation¬ wide. Thereafter, banks deemed to be in satisfactory condition were gradually authorized to reopen. The greater part of the weeding out process was a matter of weeks. At the end of the next year, 1934, the number of banks was 16,000; 12 years before it had been more than 30,000. (About 1/2)

The banking crisis of 1933 was probably the most severe ever suffered. There had been general suspensions before the Civil War, but they had not necessarily entailed closure; suspension had then meant that a bank would not redeem its obligations in gold and, silver but   continued operations otherwise. In 1933 and in the years preceding suspension meant absolute closing, which might, however, be temporary and was in most cases. But meantime it entailed a drastic stoppage of the customary means of payment. The condition affected whole regions and whole economic groups involved in the aftermath of a prolonged rise in prices and values that was inordinate and could not be sustained; it might theoretically have   been   avoided   but,   once developed, no credit institution could stop its consequences. Besides the Federal reserve system, the government revived the War Finance corporation for the purpose of agricultural financing, developed a farm-loan system with intermediate credit banks and toward the end in 1932, set up the Reconstruction Finance corporation, which lent on a larger scale to banks. It also liberalized the terms on which federal reserve banks, might lend, but all these emergency measures, though they tempered the inevitable, could not prevent it.

The problem was complicated by the fact that the agricultural depression was simultaneous with speculative booms in Florida real estate and in corporate stocks. Funds intended for relief in depressed regions found their way swiftly into speculation; and measures intended to restrain speculation threatened recovery in agriculture. In 1929 a collapse in stock-market speculation began a period of general depression lasting several years. The great weaknesses manifested in this period renewed a dormant advocacy of branch banking and also developed a variation of it in organizations comprising separate banks owned by holding companies, In the larger cities of the east and the far west, banks built up systems of numerous offices; and in many states, including notably California, branch organizations of considerable size were formed, partly by the establishment of new offices and partly by the merging of independent banks.

There was intense controversy over the question in congress, but the opponents of branch banking, who were strongest in the regions where there was no branch banking and where bank failures were most numerous, resisted successfully all attempts to do more than make federal law as liberal as state law in those states where branches were not forbidden. As a result,

banking in the United States at mid-20th century was still typically conducted by individual banks, mostly small, local and having but one office. This situation was a peculiarity   as compared with banking elsewhere in the world and as compared with other kinds of business in the United States. Yet despite the disinclination of most small banks to become units in large organizations and despite the disinclination of most large metropolitan banks to undertake the responsibilities of widespread branch systems, the ratio of the number of banks to the number of banking offices continued to raise after 1933. Though peculiarly resistant,   the   banking business seemed to be gradually yielding to a general trend toward large-scale organization. In this period unincorporated banks practically disappeared. In 1900 they numbered about 5,000, mostly very small. Though little is known of them collectively, some were important, the most famous being J. P. Morgan and Company, New York, which incorporated in 1940. The crisis of 1933 occasioned establishment of the Federal Deposit   Insurance   corporation   [F.D.I.C.],   to insure deposits in all member banks of the federal reserve system and in nonmembers which qualified. Each insured bank was to pay an annual assessment for the insurance, which   was   to cover deposits up to $5,000 (later $10,000) in each account [today it is up to $100,000]. The corporation was also authorized to take over insured banks in difficulties to rehabilitate or liquidate them. Bank failures diminished to almost nothing after 1933.

The Late 1930's and World War II.—In 1935 there, was an important reorganization of the federal reserve system, involving the federal reserve board (the legal, name of which was changed to board of governors of the federal reserve system), the federal open market committee (which thenceforth comprised the board members and five reserve bank presidents) and the management of the federal reserve banks. This change increased the authority of the board and the committee and also recognized more fully the primary importance   of   open-market operations. When the system was established in 1914. it was expected that banks in need of reserve funds would borrow from the reserve banks and that in consequence the discount rate of the reserve banks would have a regulatory effectiveness. Actually, it came about that banks were extremely reluctant to borrow. The result was that the scope of regulatory action was much diminished and the monetary authorities were left little initiative. Open-market operations—the purchase and sale of government securities by the federal reserve banks—were found to be immediately effective in augmenting or reducing the reserves of banks, and they allowed the authorities to take the initiative in regulating credit. The usefulness of open-market operations was first realized in the early 1920s but their effectiveness   depended   on   unified action by all 12 federal reserve banks. The Banking act of 1935 recognized in law the results of about 15 years' experience.

This accomplishment was already in process of being nullified, however, by the sale of gold to the United States by the rest of the world. Political and economic uneasiness in Europe was mainly responsible for the pouring of the world's gold into the United States, and its domestic effect was such an augmentation of bank reserves that regulatory powers were inadequate to offset it. The authorities were committed to an easy money policy because   they   wished   to encourage business recovery, but they could scarcely have chosen otherwise, even though they received and from time to time used, the power to require member banks to maintain larger reserves. Toward the end of the 1930s, however, preparations for war began to quicken activity decisively; there began, also, an expansion of the public debt, which raised the   total   from $45,000,000,000 in 1940 to $279,000,000,000 in 1945. A large part of the debt was acquired by banks and paid for by an increase in their deposit liabilities. Still further inflationary potentials were created when the banks sold their government obligations to the federal reserve banks and enlarged their reserves and thereby their lending power. The federal reserve   banks   were inhibited from declining to purchase the government securities because to do so would have depressed their market price, impaired the government's credit and raised the interest cost. The dilemma thus faced by the monetary authorities—whether to follow .policies primarily directed to the maintenance of low interest rates on the federal public debt or to exercise greater control over inflationary pressures—was not resolved until early 1951. In the course of the discussions leading to the resolution of the dilemma, the semi-independent status of the federal reserve sys¬ tem was brought into question in some quarters.

In March 1951, however, a joint announcement was made indicating that the treasury and the federal reserve system had reached an "agreement" with respect to the "debt management   and

monetary policies to be pursued.. ." Thereafter, the federal reserve system did exercise certain of its powers anew. During 1952 and 1953 policies looking to the control of inflation and to the restraint of credit expansion were followed. They were modified as a consequence of the mild recession of 1954 and thereafter were again strengthened in the interest of credit control until the autumn of 1957 when business conditions again suggested the desirability of further easing the flow of bank credit. There was substantial discussion in the late 1950s of the possible
establishment of a national monetary commission or other device to re-examine the banking and financial system of the United States. The multiplicity of financial agencies together with defects alleged by some to characterize the current banking system have combined to suggest a re-examination of the whole.

II. PRINCIPLES OF BANKING

The modem bank provides a wide variety of services. It usually accepts savings deposits, performing somewhat the duties of a very conservative investment trust. It is likely to rent out safe-deposit boxes, acting as a specialized type of warehouse. It may serve as the administrator of trust funds left with it under more or less restrictive contracts. It may act as   an   agent   in
furnishing a broad range of services, including such things as the purchase of travel tickets, the disbursement of dividend payments for large corporations and dealings in foreign exchange. While these activities of banks may impose great responsibility and call for   highly   trained
skills, they involve relatively little in the way of theoretical principles or if they do involve basic economic principles these are not peculiar to the institution of banking.

The theory of banking relates primarily to the operation of so called commercial banks. More specifically it is chiefly concerned with the activities of such banks as holders of deposit
accounts against which checks are drawn for the payment of goods and services. In Anglo-
Saxon countries, and in other countries where economic life is highly developed, these checks constitute the major part of the circulating medium. The term commercial bank embraces
institutions ranging from a small neighborhood bank such as is found in most medium-sized communities to a huge metropolitan institution or a widely spread organization with hundreds of branches. Activities may vary widely and may, indeed, be mainly noncommercial   in
character. The one feature which commercial banks have in common and which distinguishes them from savings banks, savings and loan associations and other financial institutions is the holding of deposits against which checks are drawn for use as a means of payment.

A. Creation of Deposits
Three different methods may be distinguished in the process of sending money. These may also be thought of as stages in the historical development of the art of lending. All three methods are practiced in the day-to-day work of a commercial bank but it is to the last that the theory of banking primarily relates.

Methods of Lending Money.—The first method of lending is that of a private capitalist or investor who lends his own funds on the promise of a later payment of interest and principal. It may be observed in the operation of a commercial bank: if a bank were to accumulate out of earnings more ready cash than it needed for its current operation and with this cash purchased government bonds, it would be practicing the first stage of the art of lending, that of lending its own money. The second method is that of an intermediary and consists of lending other people's money. It occurs, for example, when a depositor leaves funds with a bank and these funds are used to buy government bonds. The bank would then have acted as a middleman between the depositor who wished to leave cash for safekeeping and possibly for a small return and someone else who needed cash and had government bonds to sell. In such transactions as these, where there is a transfer of bonds or commercial paper to a bank, the borrower is not necessarily the one who receives the money from the bank. Unless the individual who gets the money is also expected at a later date to pay the obligation, the transaction amounts to a passing on of a debt from one creditor to another. In the above example the government is clearly, from the standpoint of the bank, the borrower. Likewise when a businessman discounts a customer's note at a bank, the bank becomes a lender not to the businessman but to his customer. The owner of a government bond who sells it to a bank, or the businessman who discounts a trade acceptance at a bank, thereby steps out of the role of lender; and the bank steps into the role of lender.

From an economic standpoint, the bank acts primarily as an intermediary in lending of the second type since it takes the money of depositors and places it at the disposal of borrowers or of those who previously occupied the position of lenders. The legal position, however, is that the bank owes the depositors; and the borrowers (i.e., the ultimate payers) owe the bank. In lending of the third type, banks furnish neither their own money nor money received from others; instead, they establish deposit credit against which the bank's customer can draw checks. These deposits are created as part of the lending operation. In the simplest case a businessman needing ready funds presents high-grade bills of exchange and asks the bank to place the proceeds to the credit of his checking account. Assuming that the bank has adequate reserves to satisfy legal requirements and disregarding for the moment complications which arise out of the presence of other banks, the bank will comply with the request for an advance, with the result that the businessman acquires an addition to his checking account and the bank acquires income-yielding assets in the form of the bills of exchange.

In some countries banks agree to honor customers' overdrafts up to a certain limit. Instead of deposits being created in advance, they arise as they are actually used. A loan by a bank and also the deposit resulting from the loan come into existence at the time the overdraft is honored. In the third type of lending, what the bank gives is not money in a physical sense but a right; namely, the right of the depositor to draw checks against the bank. The bank assumes the obligation of honoring checks up to the amount of the deposit credit thus granted. As will be seen below, this obligation imposes important limitations on the ability of banks to create such deposits. Within these limitations, however, the capacity of the banking system to bring about an expansion, and under other circumstances a contraction, of the volume of circulating medium may be very great.

Basis of Deposit Creation.—While the banking process is usually described in terms of

lending on commercial paper, the creation of deposits may occur through the purchase by banks of investment obligations such as treasury securities. The great expansion in bank deposits
which occurred in many countries during World War II came about predominantly through the

acquisition of treasury obligations by commercial banks. The banking process is essentially the same whether deposits are created against bills of exchange or investment securities. The effect on the economy and on the subsequent functioning of the monetary and banking system, however, may be very different. However they arise, the checks which are drawn against deposit credit may be used for the same purposes as currency. For the most pat deposit credits circulate throughout the economic system, moving from one account to another and from one bank to another, without actually being redeemed in currency at any time.

The way in which checking deposits may be created as part of the lending operation is the central concept of banking theory. The fact that deposits so created constitute an integral part, and in the Anglo-Saxon countries much the largest pat, of the means of payment largely
explains the strategic influence which commercial banks exercise in the functioning of the economic system. So it is that particular importance attaches to the meaning and nature of banking deposits.

The Nature of Deposits.—Contrary to the usual understanding of the word deposit, the expression bank deposit does not signify something which is physically present. A bank deposit is simply an entry on the books of a bank recording its obligation to a customer. While it may arise out of the transfer of cash or other assets to the bank, it is not itself an asset but a liability of the bank. The terms primary and derivative deposits related to the manner in which demand deposits (those bank deposits against which checks are freely drawn) originate. A primary deposit is one which aisles out of the deposit of checks or currency at a bank. The balancing item on the books of the bank is an addition to so-called nonearning assets in the form of cash or claims on other banks. A derivative deposit, on the other hand, is one which results from a loan or investment by the bank. The balancing item is an addition to the bank's earning assets under the classification of "loans and discounts" or "investments." The creation of derivative deposits, which may be thought of as identical with the third stage of the art of lending, is sometimes described as the "monetization of credit." The adjectives derivative and primary refer only to the way in which a deposit gets on the books of bank. When a derivative deposit is transferred to another account by being checked against, it becomes a primary deposit.

The distinction between primary and derivative deposits is of great importance in relation to the effect of banking operations on the total volume of circulating medium. A deposit of checks merely transfers demand deposits from one bank to another or from one checking account to another and does not alter the total. When demand deposits are created by the deposit of currency, the expansion of deposits is accompanied by an equivalent reduction in the amount of currency at the disposal of the public; the effect is to exchange one medium of payment, currency, for another, demand deposit, but not to increase the total means of payment available to the public. A primary deposit, at most, may change the form of circulating medium but does not directly alter the total volume. When derivative deposits are created, on the other hand, there is an increase in total circulating medium.

The effect of banking operations in bringing about a change in the supply of circulating medium is particularly apparent in periods of rapid expansion such as occurred in World Wars I and II and of sharp contraction such as has usually occurred in periods of severe depression.

B. Reserves and the Limitation of Deposit Creation

The basic limitation on the process of deposit creation is the necessity of maintaining reserves of currency or its equivalent. In order to provide for routine operations and to be able at all times to redeem deposits on demand, banks must have at their disposal an adequate amount of currency or its equivalent relative to the volume of their deposit liabilities. There must be enough "till money" to meet day-to-day demands and there must be additional funds on hand or on deposit with other banks to meet a sudden increase in demand for cash payments. The proportion of cash to deposit liabilities may vary from time to time and it customarily differs for different sizes and types of banks. Whatever the precise relationship of reserves to deposits and however it is determined, the necessity of maintaining adequate reserves sets the ultimate limit to the process of deposit creation.

Reserve Provisions.—In some countries, notably the United States, certain minimum ratios of reserves to deposits have been prescribed by law. In other countries, such as England, the ratió of reserves to deposit liabilities is left to the discretion of the banks themselves. Whether the ratio is established by law or custom, the creation of deposits must be halted when deposits have reached that multiple of the reserves held by banks which corresponds to the accepted ratio of reserves to deposits. Similarly, a reduction of reserves below this point would force a contraction of the amount of deposits based upon these reserves. Just as the banking system can expand deposits by a multiple of any addition to reserves, so deposits would be expected to contract by a multiple of reserves which are lost. The size of the multiple is the reciprocal of the reserve ratio. Because reserves are the basic factor limiting demand deposits, the theory of the behavior of bank deposits is essentially a theory of the determination and allocation of reserves. The ultimate restraining influence of reserves would apply in a banking system entirely devoid of laws or institutional controls. It is the key to the operation of the individual bank or of the entire system of banks. In addition, reserves are the principal basis by means of which central banks, as will be noted later, undertake to control bank credit in the interests of general economic stability.

Internal Drain.—The allocation of reserves is most clearly described in terms of the so-called internal and external drain of reserves. It is to be observed, first of all, that the presence of other banks within a banking system modifies the behavior of any individual bank within that system. This is because a bank which is one of many having mutual relations is subject to the possibility of an internal drain of reserves. By this is meant the shift of reserves from one bank to other banks in the system. It is regarded as internal because, while external to the particular bank losing/reserves, it is internal to the banking system.

The way in which internal drain controls the lending operation of a particular bank may be seen by supposing that a bank, having received additional reserve money, expands its deposits more rapidly than others in the system. It would almost immediately be subjected to a drain of reserves as checks drawn against the new deposits were exchanged for cash or deposited with other banks. Withdrawals over the counter and payments to settle balances due other banks would sharply reduce the reserves of the original bank. Because of internal drain, therefore, it is generally assumed that an individual bank can expand deposits by little more than the amount of the addition to its reserves. Provided that all reserves drawn out of the first bank were redeposit in other banks, the banking system as a whole, however, would be able to expand by approximately the full reciprocal of the reserve ratio. If the reserve ratio were 10%,   for example, total deposits could rise roughly tenfold; if 20%, they could rise about fivefold. An increase in reserves at one bank will, in any case, be shared with other banks in the system as a result of the checks drawn against the deposits created by the initial deposit of new reserve money being placed to the credit of deposit accounts in other banks.

External Drain.—The assumption that all new reserve money remains within the banking system is, of course, highly unrealistic. It is probable not only that most of the reserves will be drawn out of the original bank and into other banks but also that a part will be drained entirely out of the banking system. Such a movement of reserves is known as external drain. There are two principal places where funds may go which are withdrawn from the banking system. A certain amount of currency may be drawn out to circulate within the country and under certain circumstances reserve money may be sent out of the country to settle   foreign-exchange balances.

Both internal and external drain relate to the movement of reserves away from banks. They are the reverse of primary deposits, which represent the movement of checks or currency, and
therefore of reserves, to a bank. The same transaction would be called a primary deposit if viewed from the standpoint of the bank in which a check was deposited and internal drain if viewed from the standpoint of the bank against which it was drawn. The expressions primary deposit, internal drain and external drain, then, identify the movement of reserves to, within and from the banking system. They refer to specific operations related to the mechanics   of   the allocation of reserves. They do not, however, explain what causes the movements which they serve to designate.

Allocation of Reserves.—Reserves are allocated throughout the financial system in response to the necessity of effecting settlements between countries, regions, communities and individuals. These settlements are simply the residual of payments that result from the existing volume of business transactions and the manner in which they are carried out. If economic activity expands in a particular area more rapidly than elsewhere, the change in the relative proportion of business carried on will find its logical sequel in a correspondingly larger proportion of bank reserves concentrated in that area, and likewise of deposits based upon them. While the regional allocation of reserves will be altered by a change in the regional structure of business activity, the normal expectation is that at any given time an addition of new reserve money, no matter where it enters, will tend to be distributed throughout the financial system according to the same pattern as the existing stock of reserve money. The presumption is that at the end of a period of expansion each bank in the system will have gained reserves approximately in proportion to the size of its reserves relative to the total of reserves held by all banks in the system. This will tend to be true also of the bank which receives the original deposit of additional reserve money. Depending on its relative size, the permanent increase in its deposits might well be less than the original deposit of additional reserve money and also less than that of other banks in the system. Moreover, if two banks, one large and the other small, were to receive new reserve money in equal amounts the first bank could expect to retain a correspondingly larger proportion of the increase than the smaller bank.

Following a net gain in reserves, each bank will tend, after all adjustments have worked themselves out, to experience an expansion of demand deposits corresponding to the reciprocal of its reserve ratio. The basic factor in the analysis of the banking process, however, is not what happens to deposits but what happens to reserves. Deposits are to be thought of as a result and reserves as the governing, or at least the limiting, causal factor. Theoretically, the pattern by which reserves are distributed will also determine the pattern by which deposits are created.

C central Banking in Relation to Commercial Bank Reserves

The expansion of central banking in the 20th century was accompanied by a fundamental alteration in the composition and behavior of commercial bank reserves. Until the early years of the 20th century the reserves of commercial banks throughout most of the world consisted chiefly of gold and silver and, to a limited extent only, of the obligations of central banks. As a result of policies introduced in World War I, reserves came to consist mainly of the liabilities of central banks. Automatic forces governing the movement of commercial bank reserves became relatively less important; and monetary management, in a variety of forms but usually under the guidance of central banks, became more important.

The principal function of a central bank is to act as a stabilizer by attempting to prevent or moderate economic disturbances. In the latter part of the 19th century it came to be generally agreed that in order to maintain confidence and prevent financial panic, a central bank should stand ready at all times to lend additional cash when needed, but at a price   high   enough   to discourage less deserving borrowers. Back of this conception of the role of a central bank as lender of last resort lay the belief that in time of crisis a spirit of panic is promoted by fear of not being able to secure ready money including additional reserves for commercial banks. The ability of the central bank to discharge the function of lender of last resort was expected to give assurance that deserving borrowers could always obtain additional money when it was needed, but at the same time, that unwarranted borrowing could be effectively deterred. Provision of potential bank reserves was integrated with the use of the discount rate, at <u>one time</u> the most important instrument of credit control by central banks.

Creation of Commercial Bank Reserves.—In order to be able to provide commercial banks with additional reserves whenever it may be necessary, the central bank must be able to create reserves if called upon to do so. The manner in which this can be accomplished is by resorting to the <u>third stage</u> of the art of lending, which was described above in explaining how demand deposits may be created by commercial banks. In countries where the legal reserves   of commercial banks consist of deposits with the central bank, the creation of deposits for commercial banks, through the discounting of commercial paper, extension of advances or purchase of government obligations by the central bank, constitutes an increase in their reserves. Where reserve ratios are prescribed by law, reserves may be made available by a reduction of the legal reserve requirement. The principles involved are the same where central banks create liabilities in the form not of deposits but of bank notes, which may either circulate as currency or be used as reserves by commercial banks.

The basic factor limiting the ability of a central bank to create commercial bank reserves or

currency is similar to that which limits the ability of the commercial bank itself to create deposits; namely the necessity of maintaining reserves against its note or deposit liabilities. As in the case of commercial banks, the maximum amount of liabilities which a central bank can create on the basis of a given amount of reserves is determined by the reciprocal of its reserve ratio. The reserve ratio may be set by custom or law and is subject to modification in time of emergency. Under an international gold standard the amount of reserves was determined primarily by gold movements between countries. In the absence of a metallic standard, reserve limitations are ordinarily set by law.

The ability of central banks to create reserves greatly extends the limits of deposit expansion by commercial banks as they were described earlier. In a system where commercial banks must keep a 20% reserve and the central bank a 25% reserve, the maximum deposit expansion possible on the basis of the addition of new basic reserve money is 20 to 1 in contrast with an expansion of only 5 to 1 without the central bank. The larger figure represents a combination of the <u>third stage</u> of the art of lending both at the member bank level and at the central bank level. Credit expansion by a reciprocal of the commercial bank reserve ratio is superimposed upon credit expansion by a reciprocal of the central bank reserve ratio. Substantial as credit expansion by the commercial banks is, the possibility of expansion that can result from the action of the central bank is much greater. This feature of central banks is the source of great flexibility if it functions well, but it can also be the source of extreme inflation and deflation if it operates badly. The foregoing description of deposit creation may be summarized by noting that there are <u>three</u> distinct levels of deposit expansion. In the <u>first</u> place, a single bank can expand its deposits by little more than a 1-to-1 ratio with an addition to reserves. This is because of the loss of reserves to other banks within the system; i.e., internal drain. <u>Second</u>, the commercial banks as a group can expand collectively to the limit of the reciprocal of the reserve ratio. <u>Third</u>, the system of commercial banks together with the central bank can expand far beyond this amount, theoretically up to the limit of the reciprocal of the reserve ratio of the commercial banks multiplied by the reciprocal of the reserve ratio of the central bank.

The Control of Credit.—Probably the most familiar aspect of central banks in relation to the reserves of commercial banks has to do with the control of credit by the central bank. The principal general instruments of credit control are the making of discounts and advances at prescribed discount rates, open-market operations (i.e., purchase or sale of government securities) and changes in reserve requirements. All of these instruments represent devices for influencing the volume of commercial bank reserves. The theoretical basis on which these policies rest is that since reserves limit deposits the way to control deposits is to control reserves. Certain selective controls designed to limit particular types of credit directly, as through restricting or even prohibiting the amount of stock-market or installment credit that may be used, became familiar in the United States and various other countries after 1930. Despite substantial modifications in the art of central banking, the control of credit remained the principal method by which central banks attempted to promote economic stability, and the general methods operating through commercial bank reserves continued to be the principal means of exercising credit control. Chief reliance is likely to be upon the general instruments under relatively normal economic conditions. The selective instruments have found their greatest use in times of severe disturbance such as war.

72

The effectiveness of the general instruments of central bank control depends upon the fulfillment of certain well-defined conditions. The first of these is a governable relationship between the reserves and deposits of commercial banks. This means either the maintenance of a constant ratio or of a ratio which can be controlled by the action of the central   bank.   The second requirement for effective control of credit is the ability of the central bank to influence the volume of commercial bank reserves. In certain countries these conditions were vitiated at tines after 1930, first by the emergence of excess commercial bank reserves and later by the pursuit of policies which enabled commercial banks to obtain reserves almost at will through the sale of government securities to the central bank. The consequent impairment of the power of central banks to exercise effective control over credit   was   partly   a   reflection   of   the   more dominant place occupied by treasury policies.

P. Theory of the Banking Firm

The banker has been described as a dealer in debts. In contrast with other businessmen, he holds few assets of a tangible sot; his resources consist almost entirely of the debts of businessmen and the government. At the same time, he owes large sums in the , form of time and demand deposits. The demand deposits impose an unqualified obligation to pay in currency whenever it is requested and the time deposits, even though a short period of grace is allowed by law, are usually expected to be paid when the customer wishes. Thus, the bulk of the bank's liabilities are subject, nominally at least, to payment on call. In actual practice, of course, net payments are likely to be relatively small. It is absolutely essential, however, that the resources of the bank be managed in such a way that it can meet   all   demands   for   currency   as   they   are presented. The problem confronting any bank, therefore, is to keep the realizable value of assets equal to the bank's liabilities to depositors.

The Fundamental Banking Problem.— In practice, the fundamental banking problem may be divided into two parts, the immediate and the long run. The immediate, or short-run, problem is that of keeping liquid assets equal to liquid liabilities. The question of the liquidity of liabilities is not so much a matter of form or legal provisions as it is of the actual presentation of claims for payment in currency, or its equivalent. The short-run phase of the banking problem, in other words, is the problem of liquidity; i.e., of being able to meet all demands as they are presented. The long-run banking problem, on the other hand, is the problem of solvency. It is a question of keeping the realizable value of total assets equal to that of total liabilities; it turns on the question of ,whether the bank could be dissolved without loss to anyone.

Of the two, the short-run banking problem is the more critical. Failure to remain in a position to meet all claims as they are presented leaves the bank with no choice but to close its doors. It is synonymous with bankruptcy. The long-run problem, on the other hand, would presumably be of direct importance only if it became necessary to close out the bank. There is   a   classic instance of a Canadian bank which was technically insolvent for 40 years but continued to remain open throughout that entire time because it was able to maintain short-run liquidity and meet all claims for cash as they were presented. The long-run banking problem is likely to be of great practical significance in an indirect manner. Unless proper consideration is given to the ultimate safety of bank assets, a situation is much more likely to develop where the bank will not be able to meet the critical problem of short-run liquidity.

Policies directed toward the restriction of liabilities require much less attention from bankers and are ordinarily less important than those directed toward the maintenance of assets. In time of crisis, as during a run on a bank, banks may seek to delay presentation of claims. Attempts may be made to reassure depositors and persuade them that it is unnecessary to demand cash. Most of the paying windows may be temporarily closed and excessive time may be taken in counting out currency. Safeguards, or guarantees, may be introduced under governmental

sponsorship. More fundamental methods are also employed to restrict not the presentation but the expansion of liabilities. The most familiar of these is the imposition of legal requirements with respect to the ratio of reserves against deposit liabilities. At times the authorities have attempted with less success to enforce certain ratios of capital accounts to deposit liabilities. Certain types of bank liabilities, particularly bank notes, have been prohibited or subjected to quantitative limitation.

Portfolio Policy.—The problem of maintaining the realizable value of assets is complicated by the fact that the features which enable particular assets to satisfy banking needs may be more or less in conflict with one another. A bank which held cash equal to its deposit liabilities would be assured of meeting all demands for withdrawal but it is unlikely that such a bank would be able to cover necessary expenses, let alone show a profit. On the other hand, if it were to put all its available funds into high-yield, relatively illiquid instruments, it might find itself in a

position where it could not meet its promises to pay currency when requested to do so. Between these two extremes lies the path the successful banker must follow.

The amount of currency, or its equivalent, which a bank holds is set partly by law and partly by what experience demonstrates to be necessary for the satisfactory conduct of the business. In acquiring earning assets, a banker must constantly consider the criteria of liquidity, safety and profitability. The first of these tests is addressed primarily to the shot-run phase of the banking problem and the second to the long-run phase. Profitability ordinarily varies inversely with safety and liquidity. Portfolio, policy (i.e., the bank's policy toward various types of earning assets) is directed, therefore, to effecting a satisfactory compromise among these three criteria; i.e., to obtaining assets which are as profitable as possible while providing as great safety and liquidity as the bank considers essential.

Liquidity may be achieved through holding a security until the maturity date is reached. The so-called self-liquidating commercial paper and the short-term bills and notes of governments are customarily expected to provide liquidity in this way. An asset is also liquid, however, if it can be sold or borrowed upon at its full book value. This type of liquidity is said to depend upon shift ability. From the standpoint of the individual bank, it is immaterial whether the shifting takes place to another bank, to a central bank or to an agency of the government, except so far as the difference affects the certainty of being able to make the shift. The difference may be highly significant from the standpoint of the banking system, however, since shifting to another bank does not provide liquidity for the system as a whole. While shifting to another bank would merely transfer existing reserves, shifting to the central bank would presumably increase total bank reserves and thereby make the entire system more liquid.

E. Development of Banking Principles

What came generally to be regarded as the traditional theory of commercial banking was first clearly set forth by Adam Smith in An Inquiry Into the Nature and Causes of the Wealth of Nations (1776). This theory focuses on the part played by commercial paper and is sometimes referred to as the "real-bills doctrine." It proceeded in its simplest terms from the assumption that commercial banks would confine their lending operations to the purchase of short-term, self-liquidating bills and notes arising out of production and trade.

The Real-Bills Doctrine.—An increase in production and trade was presumed to give rise to a larger volume of bills and promissory notes. By the discount of this commercial paper at banks, demand deposits would be increased with the result that the growth in volume of business
would lead directly to a corresponding increase in the volume of circulating medium. Likewise, with declining business, fewer bills would be drawn so that as old bills matured there
would be an automatic contraction in the volume of commercial paper held by banks and with it a corresponding reduction in demand deposit. An essential part of the-theory was the so-called law of reflux, whereby any excess of deposits was expected to flow back and be canceled
through the retirement of maturing loans. Shortness of term to maturity was, in part, a device for enabling the process of reflux to operate promptly, and the necessity of paying interest was expected to provide an inducement for credit to flow back when it was no longer required. The basic assumptions of the real-bills doctrine were that the volume of commercial paper would be proportional to the volume of trade, that a roughly constant proportion of commercial paper would be presented for borrowing at the banks, and that on the basis of commercial paper alone the banks would create demand deposits. These were the fundamental features, conceptually, of a mechanism whereby the volume of circulating medium was expected to adjust automatically to the changing level of economic activity.

Not only was the real-bills doctrine a theory of the adjustment of the circulating medium to the "needs of trade" but at the same time it implied a solution to the fundamental banking problem of maintaining assets equal to liabilities. Insistence on the shot-term feature of commercial

paper was presumed to assure liquidity of assets and insistence on the self-liquidating feature was presumed to assure safety. Short-term commercial paper was regarded, then, as offering the most satisfactory means of meeting the portfolio requirements of safety, liquidity and profitability. The real-bills doctrine, as <u>Lloyd W. Mints</u> - pointed - out in his History of Banking Theory in Great Britain and the United States, had a long and influential history. It was   the

basis of the defense of the Bank of England during the restriction period from 1797 to 1821, Under the name of "the banking principle" it was widely endorsed by bankers, economists and government officials; it was a major factor in the conception, organization and early operation of the federal reserve system in the United States, The doctrine, however, was by no means free from attack. The most, significant criticism related to what <u>R. G Hawtrey</u> described   as   "the

inherent instability of bank credit." The basis of the argument was that the volume of commercial paper may vary with changes in the value rather than the physical volume of what is produced and traded, Rising prices and increasing business activity would lead, it was said, to more commercial paper and so to an expanding volume of bank deposits. The expansion of

deposits, by further raising prices, would contribute to a continuation of the upward movement of the money volume of business and the quantity of commercial paper, with a resulting
tendency toward a self-inflammatory upward spiraling of prices. Conversely, falling of prices and business activity would cause loans and discounts to decline, which would cause a
contraction of demand deposits. This destruction of circulating medium would induce a further decline of prices, business and volume of commercial paper, thus feeding a continuing
downward spiral of prices, The substance of this line of reasoning is that bank credit is not only inherently unstable but that it is unstable in a manner which is sympathetic with and conducive to swings of the business cycle.

Critics of the "real-bills doctrine" also maintained that in actual operation changes in the rate of lending by banks were likely to reflect differences in the expectations of bankers with regard to the future profitability of business rather than changes in the physical volume of business
activity. To the extent that credit standards applied by bankers varied in different phases of the business cycle, bank lending on commercial paper would not provide an accurate adjustment of deposits to the physical volume of business activity. It was also argued that, on the one hand, rigid insistence on real bills would rule out many types of productive lending which were
desirable from the standpoint of both borrower and lender and, on the other hand, paper which formally gave the appearance of being short-term and commercial might fail, in actual practice, to demonstrate these qualities. Nor was it to be assumed, in view of the changes constantly
taking place in methods of business financing, either that fluctuations in business activity would lead to corresponding variations in the volume of commercial paper or that a constant
proportion of the commercial paper that did arise would find its way to the banks.

Composition of Bank Assets.—Traditional banking theory, especially as developed along the lines of the real-bills doctrine, was not a general theory of banking. It applied to a special case; i.e., one where bank assets consisted of the particular type represented by short-term, self-
liquidating paper arising out of production and trade. In many areas, especially outside English seeking countries, the theory was never entirely applicable, and elsewhere, notably in the
United States, it became highly unrealistic after 1930 and especially after 1940. Where there is a high proportion of treasury obligations and other noncommercial securities in the portfolios of commercial banks, a situation which became general after 1930, the theory of banking as traditionally formulated requires substantial modification. The change in the composition of bank assets did not alter fundamentally the mechanical operation of the banking system or the general principles of deposit creation. It did, however, signify a change in the consequences of bank operations and in the cyclical behavior of banking.

In the first place, the different basis of deposit creation signifies a change in the economic functions performed by banks. To the extent that assets consist of treasury obligations, the credit operations of banks are no longer directly related to the production and exchange of goods and services, and banks cease to play the same part in allocating economic resources among competing users and uses that they do when making commercial loans. Moreover, since treasury obligations are assumed to have the highest credit standing, banks can hardly be said to be raising the quality of credit when they exchange their credit for that of the government. The one major function that remains substantially unchanged is that of providing, in the form of demand deposits, the principal element in the emulating medium. As part of this activity banks continue to be the center of a clearing organization by means of which payments and financial transfers are conveniently and efficiently effected throughout the economy.

Most important of all, a shift to assets of a noncommercial type implies a modification of the cyclical behavior of bank credit. This follows partly from the decline of automatism but even more from the fact that the volume of investment securities and particularly treasury obligations, unlike the volume of commercial paper, does not tend to vary directly with the total money value of business transactions. To the extent, therefore, that deposits are tied to investment securities rather than to commercial paper, the basis of the automatic adjustment of circulating medium to business activity disappears. The effect is to remove the principal reason for expecting banks to provide automatic elasticity of the money supply. By the same token, there is likewise less justification for regarding bank credit as inherently   unstable,   and particularly as unstable in a manner tending to aggravate cyclical fluctuations in business activity.

The course of banking development in the mid-20th century demonstrated the shortcomings of the real-bills doctrine as the central core of a general theory of banking. In altering the basis of banking functions and, behavior the change in character of bank portfolios also weakened the force of much of the familiar criticism of banking. The readjustment of bank portfolios away from the extreme concentration on treasury obligations that existed at the end of World War II was notable not so much for a return to earlier proportions of short-term self-liquidating
commercial paper as for the expansion of newer, noncommercial types of assets. These included term loans with a maturity often of several years, mortgages and various categories of consumer installment paper. In the course of time, then, banking theory has become   more general by becoming less narrowly identified with any specific type of asset. The composition of bank assets continues to provide a key to the operation of the banking system at any given time. It is, moreover, the most important element to be born in mind when   comparing   the banking system of one country, or one period, with that of another.

III. PRACTICE OF BANKING
The legal framework within which banks canyon their activities differs widely from country to country. In the United States there are three supervisory bodies within the federal government in addition to one in each of the 48 states. Banks are subject to detailed regulation and to close and sometimes duplicating examination. At the other extreme are the   banks   of   the   United Kingdom and the continent which, for the most part, operate under the provisions of laws governing business corporations in general and are subject to no official supervision or examination. In some countries banks are not even required to make public annual reports of their operation. While banking practices likewise differ substantially in the various countries, the contrasts are less pronounced than differences in legal status might suggest. The character of banking practices is influenced to a considerable extent by the banking organization   of   the country, depending, for example, on whether there are predominantly unit banks or branch banks and whether, or not, there is a strong central bank.

Banking Structure.-The most usual form of corporate organization is the branch banking system, which consists of a home office at some central point with branches situated elsewhere.

The number of branches may range from one or two to several thousand, and the branch system may be local or may extend over the entire country and even beyond into foreign countries. At the other extreme is the unit-bank form of organization with all of the bank's operations carried on at <u>one</u> central establishment. Where two or more banks are under common ownership, they are known as a group banking system if the ownership is vested in a holding company, and as a chain banking system if they are owned by an individual or a small group of individuals.

Outside the United States banking is carried on principally by branch banking systems. In the United States the typical form of organization is the unit bank; although the other forms are also encountered, they are less common and are not widely distributed geographically.

The capital structure of a bank includes <u>three principal</u> accounts: capital, surplus and undivided profit. The last is an operating account which is increased by current earnings and decreased by payment of certain expenses, dividends and occasionally by transfers to surplus. The other two accounts are relatively permanent. Aside from the use of these accounts in the starting of the bank, they act as a cushion to protect depositors against possible loss. Since they represent the stockholders' stake in the business, they are usually regarded as providing an inducement to

exercise care in the management of the bank. A certain amount of surplus may be paid in at the time of subscription to the original capital, and the surplus account is likely to be built   up

further out of earnings. When losses have been incurred greater than can be charged against undivided profit, they may be absorbed by transfers out of surplus account.

The administrative structure of a bank is headed by a board of directors, who ordinarily serve without direct compensation other than fees for attending meetings or for special services

performed. They are chosen for their standing in the community as well as for the breadth and variety of their business experience and their connections which may serve to attract business to the bank. They are responsible for electing officers, determining major policies of the bank and ordinarily for deciding on transactions in which relatively large sums of money are involved. The actual administration and operation of the bank are under the guidance   of   the   bank's

officers, whose numbers, duties and degrees of specialization vary greatly according to the size and character of the bank. The president, or chief executive officer (C.E.O.), is customarily on the board of directors and other officers may be. In small banks the position   of   president   is

often more or less honorary and he may serve without salary.

Deposits.—Deposits constitute the great bulk of the liabilities of banks. They ordinarily far exceed the capital accounts. Other liabilities such as unearned interest, deferred maintenance and reserve for contingencies are chiefly of an accounting character and usually are of minor proportions. It is through the holding of deposits that banks perform their most distinctive

services to the public. According to the terminology employed in the United States, deposits are of two general types: demand and time. The demand deposits, called current accounts in England and sight deposits in France, are payable in currency or by transfer via check to other banks at any time the depositor requests. In the case of time deposits, known as deposit accounts in Great Britain, the bank has a legal right, though it may not be exercised, to require notice of perhaps 15 or 30 days or even longer in advance of payment. Time deposits include not only savings deposits, which have the character of thrift accounts and are usually relatively small in size, but also deposits of businesses and others which may amount to large sums. Such deposits are sometimes evidenced by time certificates bearing specific maturity dates. These correspond to the "fixed deposits" of British banks. It is customary for banks to pay interest on time deposits but not on demand deposits. [Although today it is becoming more common].

Differences in the ownership of demand deposits are a matter of great concern in the operation of banks. Since these differences largely govern the behavior of deposits, they help   to determine the policies which a bank must follow in maintaining a liquid position; i.e., in making sure that it will always have sufficient cash to meet demands. Small personal deposits are highly stable in amounts; inward and outward payments tend to offset each other and such fluctuations in totals as do occur are mainly seasonal and can readily be anticipated   and provided for. Large deposits are much more unstable and the extent and character of variations in their amounts differ widely with the type of depositor. In general, the deposits of financial institutions such as banks and insurance companies are subject to greater and more sudden fluctuations than those of other types of corporate depositors. Other large deposits may vary seasonally or with particular business transactions, such, for   example,   as   the   purchase   of additional rolling stock by a railroad company, which the officers of the bank are often able to lean about in advance. Large corporate depositors sometimes keep their banks informed of impending requirements. Similarly, in the United States the treasury gives advance notice of expected withdrawals, something that can readily be done since funds are left with banks only for safekeeping, actual payments being made against deposits at the federal reserve banks.

Large deposits may become particularly volatile in periods of uncertainty and fear. It is deposits of this type rather than the small deposits of individuals that are likely to be withdrawn first when doubt arises concerning the future solvency of a bank. This may be partly because of the greater amount which a large depositor has at stake but is probably chiefly   because   such depositors pay more careful attention to such matters and are in a position to be better informed.

Practices With Respect to Deposits.—Banks often devote great attention to the character of the-deposits they carry and to their possible future behavior. In addition, it may be the practice for the bank's comptroller or some other operations officer to be notified the moment a large check is presented for payment. The Purpose of such notification is to assist in   enabling   the bank to provide adequate cash to meet all demands without maintaining greater liquidity than is needed, since this would have the effect of encroaching on income. The amount of earning

assets a bank can own is directly related to the total of its deposit liabilities. Consequently, a strong incentive exists for attempting to expand deposits. Efforts to attract and retain deposit balances may take the form of advertising and direct negotiation, providing various types of free service and appointing influential businessmen to the bank's board of directors. At one time it was customary for banks to compete for deposits by means of the rate of interest paid on

them. This form of competition carries the danger of unduly increasing the costs of banking operations. To the extent that it merely results in taking deposits away from other banks without expanding the total of all deposits, costs may be raised with no corresponding benefit to the banking system as a whole. Because it was felt that the effect of such a practice might be to weaken the banking system, governments intervened in some countries to restrict the payment of interest on deposits. In the United States, for example, banks are no longer forbidden to pay interest on demand deposits and are limited as to the rate that may be paid on time deposits.

Banks may also require or expect depositors to maintain certain minimum or average balances in their deposit accounts. Loans may be granted upon the understanding that the borrower will leave 20% or 25% of the loan on deposit at all times. Such practices help to assure that the cost of operating the account will be met and increase the stability of deposit liabilities. The handling of deposit accounts involves a great amount of rather mechanical, routine work in connection with scrutinizing and counting coins and other currency and with sorting, recording and

distributing checks drawn on the bank itself and on other banks. Much of this work can be carried out with the aid of highly complex machines. In banks located in smaller communities most check transactions pass directly through the hands of paying and receiving tellers. In large city banks most of them may be conducted by mail. A bank may assume the task of receiving and crediting directly to the customer's deposit account payments for dividends, interest, bills receivable and the like, supplying the customer with a detailed record of the transactions handled by the bank. The work of handling mail deposits and of the transit department, which receives and forwards checks, is usually on a continuous basis day and night, seven days a week. [24/7].

Lending Operations.—The granting of loans to business borrowers has traditionally been regarded as the primary basis of commercial banking. During the first half of the 20th century and especially in the 1930s and 1940s, the extension of bank credit through purchase of

investment securities by banks became increasingly common while the granting of commercial and industrial loans declined in relative importance. Investments generally carry a lower rate of return than loans but the work entailed in making investments is less than in granting and administering loans. A bank may lend on a promissory note which bears interest until the note is due. It may also lend on drafts or acceptances which are in the form of noninterest-bearing obligations to pay a stipulated sum of money at some future time. Little distinction is made between the two types and they are ordinarily combined in a common account called "loans and discounts." When a bank acquires a noninterest-bearing obligation, it calculates the proceeds by subtracting from the face value a sum equal to interest on this amount from the date of purchase to maturity, a procedure known as "discounting." The fact that interest is deducted in advance makes the net rate on the sum actually lent by the bank slightly higher than the nominal rate.

It is a common practice for banks to grant their regular customers a "line of credit" under which the bank agrees to extend loans up to a certain maximum when requested to do so, subject, of course, to the meeting of certain specified conditions. The potential borrower can carry out his business plans with greater assurance because of the knowledge that he will be able to obtain funds quickly when they are needed. Banks use to require a customer to maintain a deposit balance of from 10% to 25% of the line of credit granted. This practice is frequently criticized and is by no means universal. Borrowers sometimes pay a small interest charge, amounting to perhaps Vi % of the unused part of the line of credit, under so-called "stand-by" agreements. A slightly different practice, common in Great Britain and a few other countries, is to grant customers an overdraft privilege. Under this arrangement the bank agrees to honor drafts up to a specified amount and charges interest on such overdrafts until they are paid off. Where this method is used, the overdraft privilege becomes a means of granting loans automatically and without separate formality as they are desired.

Larger banks maintain departments of substantial size for soliciting and servicing loans. New business departments engage aggressively in competing for loans and in seeking opportunities for the extension of credit. Credit departments maintain extensive files on the credit standing of actual and potential customers. Officers of the bank may furnish financial counsel and the bank may supply the services of technical experts to advise on plans designed to increase the operating efficiency of the borrower's business. Sometimes such assistance is related to the provision of additional credit by the bank or to the safeguarding of past loans. At other times it is designed to strengthen good will by promoting the customer's prosperity.

Types of Loans.—At one time bank lending was largely confined to short-term, self-liquidating paper arising out of actual business transactions. The maturity of such paper was usually from
30 days to 6 months, or somewhat longer in the case of agricultural operations. Through the granting of renewals, the credit might, in actual practice, be extended for a much longer period of time. Many bankers adhered to the so-called "golden rule" of banking by requiring customers to clear up their indebtedness to the bank at least once a year. Others were less strict; there are records of loans which were nominally of a short-term character but which had   a
continuous life, through renewals and extensions, of 25 years or longer. Other types of loans are also commonly granted by commercial banks. Term loans have a maturity longer than that of the ordinary commercial and industrial loan. They usually run not less than I year and may run
15 years or even longer. In the case of term loans running more than five' years, the loan contract may be divided with banks taking the earlier period of the loan and an investor of some other type taking the later period. Term loans may be used to provide working capital but are more likely to be used to pay for fixed capital, modernize equipment, obtain rolling stock and the like. Such loans may be drawn in such a manner as to permit changes to be made within the life of the loan, as by shortening or extending the time to maturity or expanding the loan to meet supplementary requirements. Term loans are usually of the amortizing type with current installments applied both to payment of interest and gradual reduction of principal.

Considerable flexibility and variety have been introduced into lending practices. For example, loans may be granted for the construction of tankers with provision for the payment of interest and principal out at the earnings of the ships. Loans of this sort are often extended jointly by commercial banks and long-term investors such as insurance companies. Again, loans are sometimes made on security of underground oil reserves, payment being provided for through the gradual pumping and sale of the oil.

Various types of collateral may be pledged as security for loans granted by banks. The most familiar types of collateral are real estate, stocks and bonds and bills of lading, warehouse receipts and trust receipts. The market value of the collateral at the time the loan is made is always expected to be substantially greater than the face value of the loan and provision is often made for posting additional collateral if necessary to protect this so-called "margin." Collateral

81

loan agreements ordinarily permit the borrower to substitute different collateral of suitable amount and quality in place of the collateral originally pledged. This feature is designed to protect the borrower against possible loss through inability to sell or against being deprived of possible gain if a favorable time to sell should occur, either of which might happen if the collateral were completely immobilized for the duration of the loan. While the collateral pledged against outstanding loans is subject to continuous scrutiny, the attention devoted to it is particularly close during periods of weakness in the markets with which the collateral is concerned. Likewise the size of the margin required many be increased to provide against the possibility of sharp price declines. In addition, central bank authorities may stipulate increased margin requirements with a view to restricting the volume of credit extended for use in the stock market.

With the expanded use of relatively expensive durable goods, such as automobiles and household appliances, the banks gradually tuned to lending for consumption purposes. Techniques were devised for insuring the automobile or other durable consumer goods against theft or damage during the life of the loan, and for seizure and sale of the article purchased in case of default. Banks also entered the field of so-called personal loans, usually made for such purposes as medical expenses, education and the consolidation of indebtedness. Loans of this sort are ordinarily granted without the pledge of specific collateral and without requiring a cosigner of the note.

Repayment of both consumer and personal loans is typically provided for by a series of uniform payments which combine payment of interest with amortization of the principal. The debt may be represented by a book of coupons, each of which represents one of the payments due, the coupon being torn out and receipt acknowledged on the stub at the time the payment is made. Consumer and personal loans proved profitable to banks, despite the relatively high costs of operation resulting from the small sums involved in each individual transaction and the large amount of administrative detail. Rates, although considerably below those charged on similar loans by most other lenders, are higher than on other bank assets. Banks in larger communities maintain separate consumer credit and personal loan departments and engage in extensive advertising and promotional activities to expand this type of business. Banks furnish credit to their competitors in these fields by lending to companies which specialize in the granting of consumer and personal loans. Furthermore, while rates charged by banks on consumer and personal loans are in general the highest received by banks, the rates charged consumer finance and personal finance companies are among the lowest.

Rates.—As has been indicated, the rates charged by banks on different types of loans vary substantially. The principal factor in such differences appears to be the size of the loan, though the type of the loan, which is likely to be closely related to size, is also an important consideration. Customers who borrow in large amounts, such as finance companies, large industrial corporations and transportation companies, are likely to enjoy a high credit standing. Furthermore, the tact that the sums involved are so large usually means that the costs of administration are small when calculated on a percentage basis. There is the further tact that large borrowers find it easy to tap alternative sources of credit so that a bank must offer as favorable terms as possible if it is to attract and retain their business.

The relation of collateral to rates charged by banks is somewhat ambiguous. Security loans, which consist chiefly of collateral loans to brokers dealing in securities, carry it low rate of interest. This is particularly true of call loans, which are subject to payment whenever   the lender demands. Other types of collateral loans, on the other hand, are likely to carry a relatively high rate of interest. This may be explained largely on the ground, that where a borrower's credit position is weak added protection may be demanded in the form of collateral. It is not that collateral makes a loan weak, but that a weak loan may require the further strengthening which collateral affords. Somewhat similarly, loans bearing one signature ordinarily command a lower rate of interest than loans requiring a cosigner because only loans of the very highest credit standing are issued on a single signature.

Bank rates show considerable variation along regional and geographical lines. They are typically much higher on the average in rural areas than in cities, and are higher in the small cities than in the large. These differences are accounted for to a minor extent on grounds of differences in risks or degree of competition among lenders, but are chiefly attributable   to differences in size of loans. It happens that geographical differences in rates tend to coincide with differences in average size of loans; loans are generally smaller in the country than in cities, and in small cities than in large. When allowance is made for the factor of size of loan, regional differences in rates charged by banks (within a particular country, of course) appear to be relatively slight.

Investing Practices.—The form in which banks extend credit has always been influenced by the nature of the economy in which they operate, and especially by the apparent credit needs of the community and the methods of supplying those needs. It was natural that in England, where the traditional conception of commercial banking grew up during the 18th and 19th centuries, great emphasis should have been placed upon the short-term commercial   loan.   In   a   trading nation it was working capital that was chiefly needed and there was an abundance of foreign and domestic bills of exchange which could be used in providing such capital.

In other countries the same degree of concentration on commercial paper was never feasible, and other types of credit instruments played a correspondingly larger pat in the operations of banks. Even in Great Britain and other Anglo-Saxon countries where the British conception of commercial banks exerted greatest influence, holdings of longer-term securities   of   the investment type came to occupy an important place in the portfolios of banks. The shift toward investments was stimulated by the great expansion in governmental financing which characterized World Wars I and II and the severe depression of the early 1930s. It was influenced, no doubt, by disturbances of world trade and changes in the financing methods of business which entailed a decline in the relative volume and availability of commercial paper. Because real-estate mortgages are usually issued for fairly long periods of time and no general market for them characteristically exists, they were usually regarded as unsuitable for purchase by commercial banks. Accordingly, such investments were either prohibited or restricted. In the course of time, however, government guarantees, together with greater use of the amortization feature, tended to reduce somewhat the illiquidity of mortgages   and   thereby   to   increase   the popularity among banks of investments of this character.

<u>Types of Investments.</u>—Investment in mortgages may be limited to some prescribed ratio of capital and surplus or of time deposits. As in the case of other types of assets, such as common stocks or real estate itself, the limit may be exceeded temporarily if the asset is acquired   to protect a loan or investment previously made. There is a tendency for certain types of restricted assets to constitute a larger proportion of the earning assets of banks in depressions   than   in good times. This is partly because commercial and other loans decline more rapidly than other types of assets in a period of falling business. It is also influenced by the fact that banks are likely to acquire, as a result of default, collateral which was pledged as security on   loans granted earlier.

The principal types of investments held by banks are mortgages, government obligations and corporate bonds. In the United States ownership shares in corporations are ordinarily not held by banks except to the extent that they may have been acquired to protect a loan previously made, and when this has occurred it is expected that the security so acquired will be sold as soon as can be done without undue scarifies. Government obligations are by far the   most important category of bank investments. They consist predominantly of securities of the federal government, but obligations of provincial or local units of government, sometimes called "municipals," (or muni's) may also be included. Investments in treasury obligations include a wide range of securities. Typically they may be thought of as embracing shot-term securities with maturities of from 3 months to a year, intermediate securities with maturities up to 5 years and bonds with maturities up to 25 years or even longer. While banks   may   hold   a   limited proportion of their assets in the issues having the longest maturities they tend to concentrate their holdings overwhelmingly in the shorter-term issues. It would be wholly erroneous, therefore, to regard the investments of commercial banks as being made up of relatively illiquid long-term issues.

Problems and Policies.—The holding of investments of a longer-term character gives rise to a number of distinctive problems and policies. Certain investments, such as mortgages, may possess little or no marketability so that the bank must ordinarily plan on retaining them until maturity. A bank can safely afford to hold a certain amount of <u>illiquid</u> earning assets since, even though all of its deposits may be payable on demand, it will not be required to liquidate more than a small proportion of its assets at any one time. Some of its other long-term assets may be shift able to other lenders in case a bank requires greater liquidity. The disadvantage that at the very time when one bank wants to sell other banks may not be willing to buy is partially overcome in situations where the central bank undertakes to support the securities market; the lack of shift ability to other banks may then be made up by shift ability to the central bank. One of the most important devices for counteracting the illiquidity inherent in long-term assets is that of spacing maturities. By regularly acquiring bonds having a maturity of five years, a bank will come to have in the course of time a block of securities averaging half that length of time to maturity. Even though all the securities had a maturity of five years at the time of purchase, one-fifth of them at any time will have a maturity of one year or less and none but those just bought will have a maturity as long as five years. Spacing permits the bank to realize the yield that goes with a longer maturity while achieving much of the liquidity that goes with a shorter maturity.

Ownership of relatively long-term investments exposes a bank to the risk of fluctuations in the market value of these securities as changes occur in the level of interest rates. A fall in the market price of a particular security would impair its liquidity but would not necessarily affect its safety. It follows that by holding until maturity a bank can avoid loss of principal on securities that experience a decline in market value, provided that that security is entirely safe. This consideration, and with it the presumption in favor of a policy of holding to maturity, is especially important in respect to investments of the highest quality; in the case of treasury obligations in particular, repayment in full at date of maturity is presumably never in question. It applies to other investments as well, in the sense that the possibility of loss is greatly influenced by the bank's own decision with respect to selling.

From an operations standpoint the greatest single advantage of investments is that the bank is not dependent on borrowers coming to ask for loans. Whenever a bank has funds available for lending it can take the initiative by going out and purchasing securities in the open market. At the same time, changes in interest rates, analysis of security values and market psychology are matters of increased concern to banks. Larger banks maintain separate bond departments and carry out elaborate statistical and analytical investigations. In addition, banks in general make use of various, statistical and advisory services which specialize in providing information
bearing on the security market.

Maintenance of Liquidity and Solvency.—Some of the devices maintaining liquidity have already been indicated. The first recourse when payment is demanded by depositors is the vault cash regularly carried by the bank. A bank may also draw upon its legal reserves, even reducing them below legal requirements, subject to certain limitations on its freedom (as, for example, to make loans or declare dividends) as long as reserves are deficient. Banks which have deposits with other correspondent banks may draw on these deposits to meet unexpected demands upon them. These immediate cash resources-may be supplemented by the liquidation of certain
earning assets. Investments consisting of short-term treasury obligations are likely to be the most liquid assets, other than cash, which a bank possesses. They are the principal element in so-called secondary reserves. Largely because of the desire of banks to retain and increase their commercial loans, by reason both of their profitability and of their possible effect in bringing other business to the bank, commercial paper is not likely, in actual practice, to be treated as a secondary reserve. Methods also exist whereby funds may be temporarily shifted, on payment of a relatively small interest charge, from a bank with excess reserves to one with a reserve deficiency.

Securities in a bank's portfolio are ordinarily spaced in such a way as to provide a steady inflow of cash through the simple maturing of loans and investments. Certain loans, specifically loans to brokers secured by stock-market collateral, may be redeemable on call. It may be possible to sell short-term assets in the open market, to other banks or to the central bank with little or no sacrifice. Or a bank may elect to borrow from other banks or the central bank on its own promissory note, pledging certain of its assets as collateral for the loan. In general, tradition against borrowing by banks tends to hold borrowing to a minimum and to lead to the prompt repayment of loans by banks in case they are made. As a safeguard not so much of liquidity as

85

of solvency, loans to a bank's officers are likely to be strictly limited by law or custom. In the United States loans to a single borrower are restricted to 10% of the bank's capital and surplus, with some extension of the limit under certain conditions. In some jurisdictions provision is made for the separation of assets held against time deposits. The purpose of this practice is to prevent the withdrawal of deposits which are payable on demand from leading to the exhaustion of the best assets. Otherwise, time deposits might be left with only inferior assets behind them when the time came that they were eligible to be paid.

Banks frequently accumulate what are known as concealed assets by witting down certain
assets, such as the bank building, to an insignificant value by charge-offs against undivided profit. At a later time depreciation of loans or investments could then be equalized on the bank's books by witting up the value of the property to something closer to its actual worth. A similar result may be achieved by establishing contingency reserves to be used for writing off possible losses on loans and investments. Investments acquired at a premium, or other assets on which a future decline in value seems possible, may be written down to a lower figure by charging off certain amounts against current income. Under certain circumstances a considerable tax saving may be realized by following this practice.

Relations With Other Financial Institution.—In countries with a strong central bank the reserves of commercial banks are likely to consist largely of deposits at the central bank. In the United States the legal reserves of member banks take the form exclusively of deposits with the federal reserve banks. In other countries, and in the United States for nonmember banks,
deposits with other banks may usually be counted as reserves. In some counties deposits in banks abroad may also, within certain limits, be included as reserves.

Banks perform many services for other banks. The central bank and even larger commercial banks may occupy the position of bankers' banks. In this capacity they may discount commercial paper, make advances in the form of loans and assist in the clearing and collection of checks. Correspondent banks frequently supply credit data and other financial information, They may act as agents in providing foreign exchange and in the purchase of securities   for
other banks or their customers. These are but a few of the services which banks may afford one another. They may also share in the granting of loans, as where a particular loan is larger than one bank would be able or willing to grant alone. Banks may organize for mutual benefit into such national groups as the bankers' associations of the United States and   Canada   which
sponsor exchange of information, research on operational and policy matters and extensive educational programs. The syndicate of banks in France goes so far as to set interest rates paid on deposits. In the United States county, or regional, clearinghouse associations may undertake to establish standards with respect to banking practices, as in the determination of service
charges to be imposed by the member institutions. Upon occasion, members of clearinghouse associations have rallied to the aid of banks which were in difficulties or have taken other steps to meet conditions of crisis. In countries where banking is predominantly in the hands of a small number of large branch banking systems there is presumably   less   occasion   for   the
organization of bankers' associations such as exist in the United States.

Conditions of Competition.—The nature and extent of competition among banks, and between banks and other financial institutions, are greatly influenced by the character of the financial organization of a country. Where banking is confined to a relatively narrow field of operations, as was long traditional in Great Britain, there are fewer points of contact, competitively speaking, with other types of lending institutions than where banks engage in a wide variety of lending activities. Banks of the so-called "department-store" type such as is common in the United States may find themselves in competition with trust companies, mutual savings banks, investment counselors, consumer finance companies and investment trusts, to name but a few. One effect of the extension of banking operations into a wider area was to bring about increased competition with other financial institutions. To some extent, increased competition resulted from the entry of other lending institutions into fields already occupied by banks.

Where there are a few large branch banking systems, competition is different, though not necessarily less keen, from what it is where there are a great number of unit banks. In relations with other banks, banks have tended to avoid such forms of competition as the payment of higher rates on deposits or the acceptance of lower rates on loans, and to rely more on providing special services or other accommodation. In certain continental European counties, notably France, Germany and the Netherlands, the lines of demarcation between commercial and investment banking are not at all sharply defined. Assets may not only include securities of an investment character; banks in the Netherlands and Germany sometimes hold stock market membership, while German banks may hold shares in business enterprises and participate in their management. Similar practices are followed in other countries, even to the extent of banks specializing in particular types of businesses. The central banks of many countries deal directly with the public. Where this is the case banks are likely to find themselves in competition with the central bank. In the United States the federal reserve banks are authorized to lend to private borrowers but the field of such operation is so restricted, and their amount so small, that no significant competition can be said to have existed.

Bankers are likely to feel that their interests are threatened by an expansion of the lending activities of the government. The probability of injurious competition from this source is presumably greatest in the fields of agricultural and real-estate credit. The amount of actual competition with banks cannot be judged precisely. In certain cases banks benefit directly or indirectly by the lending activities of the government. Perhaps the principal basis of the opposition of bankers to lending by governmental agencies is the danger they see in it of an unwarranted trend toward socialism.

Customer Relationships.—Banks maintain important customer relationships with other financial institutions. They are a major source of the credit employed by investment bankers, brokers, finance companies and others. The bill broker (q. v.), who occupies a particularly strategic position in the functioning of the London money market, relies heavily on commercial banks for the credit used in his business. Governmental lending agencies may be financed in part by securities sold to banks. Banks may be the purchasers of securities sold by investment bankers and brokers and of bills sold by commercial paper houses.

The sharing of loans with other banks has already been mentioned. Banks may lend on a participating basis whereby a governmental lending agency provides part of the loan. The

guarantee by a governmental department of export credits or of a credit for military expenditures in time of war may enable a bank to undertake commitments that would otherwise be regarded as too risky. In the United States the guarantee of mortgages by the Federal
Housing administration lifted this category of real-estate obligations into a class virtually as high as that of government bonds and so made them acceptable to banks and other conservative lending institutions. At times banks have found it advantageous to shift certain   assets   to government lending agencies, thereby increasing their ability to extend other kinds of loans.

Still another type of sharing transaction Occurs where a bank and an insurance company participate jointly in extending a term loan. In such cases it is usual for the bank to take that part of the loan which involves a shorter commitment and for the insurance company to take the part having the longer maturity. Such an arrangement makes it possible for the borrower   to obtain a single loan of the size and terms he finds appropriate and for each of the lenders to satisfy its particular requirements with respect to liquidity and yield.

Overseas connections may be maintained through relations with other financial institutions. Some banks, notably in the United States, and certain large private banks have   overseas branches. Leading dominion and colonial banks are likely to have offices in London. Such overseas connections may serve as contacts for banks of the countries where they are located. Banks may carry on foreign business through foreign correspondents or affiliates. The British maintain a number of overseas banks which usually have their headquarters in London but conduct the bulk of their business in some foreign country or countries.

AMERICANA
SERIES
VANISHING CLASSICS COLLECTION

1943 Steel Penny

Buffalo Nickel

Walking Liberty Half Dollar

Mercury Dime

Standing   Liberty   Quarter

88

Indian Head Penny

Barber
Dime

Liberty Nickel
Barber Half Dollar
Barber Quarter

PRESIDENT
S
COLLECTIO
N

Lincoln Penny

Jefferson

Nickel

Kennedy Half

Dollar

Washington

Quarter

Roosevelt

Dime

Dollar

CHAPTER V

CHAPTER V
Money and God

I. ATTITUDES TOWARD MONEY AND POSSESSIONS

1. Whatever good things we have are gifts from God.

For example:

Deuteronomy 8:17, 18 — Wealth and power to get it. God to Israel: 17 Then you say in your heart, 'My power and the might of my hand have gained me this wealth.' 18 And you shall remember the LORD your God, for it is He who gives you power to get wealth...

I Chronicles 29:11-16— Riches, honor, strength, building materials.
David praying just before Solomon's accession to the throne: 11...or all that is in heaven and in earth is Yours; Yours is the kingdom, O LORD, and You are exalted as head over all. 12 Both riches and honor come from You, and You reign over all. In Your hand is power and might; in Your hand it is to make great and to give strength to all. 14 But who am I, and who are my people, that we should be able to offer so willingly as this? For all things come from You, and of Your own we have given You. 16...all this abundance that we have prepared to build You a house...is from Your hand, and is all Your own.

Ecclesiastes 5:18-20 — Wealth and good health to eat and enjoy life.
Solomon speaking in his old age: 19 As for every man to whom God has given riches and wealth, and given him power to eat of it, to receive his heritage and rejoice in his labor—this is the gift of God.

I Timothy 4:3-5 — All kinds of food.
3...foods which God created to be received with thanksgiving by those who believe and know the truth. 4 For every creature of God is good, and nothing is to be refused, f it be received with thanksgiving.

I Timothy 6:17 — All things to enjoy.
Command those who are rich in this present age not to be haughty, nor to trust in uncertain riches but in the living god, who gives us richly all things to enjoy.

James 1:17 — Everything good that we have.
Every good gift and every perfect gift is from above, and comes down from the Father of lights...

"To value riches is not to be covetous. They are the gift of God, and like every gift of his, good in themselves, and capable of a good use. But to overvalue riches, to give them a place in the heart which God did not design them to fill, this is covetousness. "
                                                                    - Herman Wayland, 1830-1893.

2. Believers are stewards over God's possessions, not independent owners.

Leviticus 19:23-25
    God directed Israel about when they were free to eat the fruit of the land because it was His.

Leviticus 25:1-7
    The land which 1 give you was to be rested every seventh year for the Lord.

Leviticus 25:8-31
    The land was God's (v. 23), therefore to be rested and returned to original owner every fiftieth year; all sales to be reckoned until the year of jubilee.

Leviticus 25:35-38
    Usury was not to be charged to a poor brother - i.e., since it was all God's.

Leviticus 25:39-46
    A poor man could not become a bond-servant to another Jew, since they were all God's servants (v.42,43).

Leviticus 25:47-55
    An Israelite bought by a Gentile could be redeemed by a relative; if not, he was to be set free at the jubilee, since he was God's servant (v. 55).

1 Chronicles 29: 14-16
    David acknowledged that all the materials he had gathered for the temple-building belonged to God.

Ezekiel 7:20,21
    God condemned Israel for using their silver and gold to make images for worship.

Haggai 2:8
    "The silver is Mine, and the gold is Mine," says the LORD of hosts.

Matthew 22:21
    Render therefore to Caesar the things that are Caesars, and to God the things that are Gods.

Matthew 25:14-29
    Parable of the talents, illustrating the responsibility of servants for possessions, and our responsibility as God's stewards.

Acts 2:44,45

Believers in Jerusalem gave up private ownership out of love. Also 4:32-35.

1 Corinthians 6: 19,20

19 Or do you not know that your body is the temple of the Holy Spirit who is in you, whom you have from God, and you are not your own ? 20 For you were bought at a price.

3. Material things should not be a goal in life.

2 Chronicles 1:11,12

11 And God said to Solomon: "Because this was in your heart, and you have not asked riches or wealth or honor...but have asked wisdom and knowledge for yourself, that you may judge My people...; 12 Wisdom and knowledge are granted to you; and I will give you riches and wealth and honor, such as none of the kings have had who have been before you...

Job 31 :24-28

Job recognized that pride in wealth is denial of God. He says: 24 If I have made gold my hope, or have said to fine gold, you are my confidence; 25 If I rejoiced because my wealth was great, and because my hand had gained much; 27 so that my heart has been secretly
enticed...28 This also would be an iniquity worthy of judgment, for I would have denied God who is above.

Proverbs 10:2

Treasures of wickedness profit nothing: but righteousness delivers from death.

Proverbs 11:4

Riches do not profit in the day of wrath, but righteousness delivers from death.

Proverbs 13:7

There is one who makes himself rich, yet has nothing; and one who makes himself poor, yet has great riches.

Proverbs 15: 16

Better is a little with the fear of the LORD, than great treasure with trouble. Also 28:6.

Proverbs 22: 1 ,2

1 A good name is to be chosen rather than great riches, loving favor rather than silver and gold. 2 The rich and the poor have this in common, the LORD is the maker of them all.

Proverbs 23:4,5

4 Do not overwork to be rich; because of your own understanding, cease! 5 Will you set your eyes on that which is not? For riches certainly make themselves wings; they flyaway. . .

Zephaniah 1: 18
Neither their silver nor their gold shall be able to deliver them in the day of the Lords wrath.

Matthew 4:8-10
Jesus refused to worship Satan even when He was offered all the kingdoms of the earth, and the glory that went with them.

Matthew 6: 19-34
We are not to worry about material things as the unsaved do, but seek God's will first and He will care for our needs. Also Luke 12:22-34.

Matthew 16:26
For what is a man profited if he gains the whole world, and loses his own soul? Or what will a man give in exchange for his soul?

Luke 12:15
Take heed and beware of covetousness: for one's life does not consist in the abundance of the things he possesses.

Luke 12:16-21
Parable of bigger barns.

1 Timothy 3:3,8
A bishop (pastor) or deacon must be one who is not greedy of filthy lucre.

1 Timothy 6:6-8
6 But godliness with contentment is great gain. 7 For we brought nothing into this world, and it is certain we can carry nothing out. 8 And having food and clothing, with these we shall be content.

Hebrews 10:34
Persecuted believers are commended for taking joyfully the spoiling of their goods, knowing that they have better possessions in heaven.

Hebrews 13:5
Let your conduct [way of life] be without covetousness, and be content with such things as you have. For He Himself has said, "I will never leave you nor forsake you."

4. Money is entrusted o believers for use as God purposes.

Three uses seem to be especially emphasized in Scripture: (1) the care of one's family, (2) the needs of others, (3) the furtherance of the Gospel message.
Note the following, but also consider many other passages included in this chapter.

Mark 7:9-13-family

Jesus rebuking the Pharisees for giving their traditions first place over God's commands: 10 For Moses said, 'Honor your father and your mother... 11 But you say, 'If a man says to his father or mother, "Whatever profit you might have received from me is Corban   [that   is, dedicated to the temple] 12 and you no longer let him do my thing for his father or his mother;
13 making the word of God of no effect through your tradition... In other words, the Lord was saying that giving to God what should go to parents was Sin.

1 Timothy 5:4,8,16 - family

8 But f anyone does not provide for his own, and especially for those of his household, he has denied the faith and is worse than an unbeliever.

Deuteronomy 15: 1 0,11 - others

10 You shall surely give to him, and your heart should not be grieved when you give to him, because for this thing the LORD your God will bless you in all your works and in all to which you put your hand. 11 For the poor will never cease from the land; therefore / command you, saying, 'You shall open your hand wide to your brother, to your poor and your needy, in your land.'

Ephesians 4:28 - others

Let him who stole steal no longer, but rather let him labor, working with his hands what is good, that he may have something to give him who has need.

Philippians 4: 1 0-19 - the ministry of the Word

Paul expresses appreciation for the support of the Philippians church for his ministry.

Matthew 6: 19,33 - the accomplishment of God's will

19 Do not lay up for yourselves treasures on earth... 20 but lay up for yourselves treasures in heaven... 33 But seek first the kingdom of God and His righteousness...

5. God is the supplier of material needs for those who trust Him.

2 Chronicles 31 :5, 1 0

There was plenty to eat when Israel turned to the Lord, bringing their tithes and offerings. Also Ecc.3:13.

Ezra 8:21-23

God provided protection from enemies and safety in travel when His people asked, in preparation for their return to the land. Also Ps. 37:25.

Psalm 128

To those that fear the Lord, God promises food, happiness, a fruitful wife and wholesome children.

Matthew 6:25-34

33 But seek first the kingdom of God and His righteousness, and all these things shall be added to you. Also Luke 12:22-34.

Hebrews 13:5,6

5 Be content with such things as you have. For He Himself has said, "I will never leave you nor forsake you." 6 So we may boldly say: "The Lord is my helper; I will not fear. What can man do to me. "

6. Money will not buy spiritual blessings.

Isaiah 55:1-3

Ho! Everyone who thirsts, come to the waters; and you who have no money, come, buy and eat ....

Ezekiel7:19

Their silver and their gold will not be able to deliver them in the day of the wrath of the LORD; they will not satisfy their souls. . .

Mathew 19:21-24

Assuredly, I say to you that it is hard for a rich man to enter the kingdom of heaven

Acts 8: 18-22

20 But Peter said to him [Simon], "Your money perish with you, because you thought that the gift of God could be purchased with money!... 21 for your heart is not right in the sight of
God..... 22 Repent therefore ....

1 Peter 1:18,19

18...you were not redeemed with corruptible things, like silver or gold... 19 But with the precious blood of Christ, as of a lamb without blemish and without spot.

7. Attitude toward money is an index of one's general attitude.

Haggai 1 :2-4

God reprimands Israel for building beautiful private homes and neglecting God's house and worship.

Matthew 6: 19- 21

19 Do not lay up for yourselves treasures on earth... 20 but layup. . . treasures in heaven... 21 For where your treasure is, there your heart will be also.

Mathew 18:23-35 (esp. v. 33)

The story of the servant for whom much was forgiven, but who refused to forgive others what they owed.

Luke 12:33,34

33 Sell what you have and give alms; provide yourselves money bags which do not grow old, a treasure in the heavens that does not fail, where no thief approaches nor moth destroys.

34 For where your treasure is, there your heart will be also.

Luke 16:10,11

10 He who is faithful in what is least is faithful also in much; and he who is unjust in what is least is unjust also in much. 11 Therefore if you have not been faithful in the unrighteous mammon, who will commit to your trust the true riches? Also v. 12.

2 Corinthians 8:3-5

(Paul speaking of the churches of Macedonia:) 3 ... they were freely willing; 4 imploring us with much urgency that we would receive the gift... 5 And this they did, not as we had hoped, but first gave themselves to the Lord, and then to us by the will of God.

8. True prosperity depends on obedience to God and favor from Him.

Genesis 39:2-5

2 The LORD was with Joseph, and he was a successful man...3 And his master saw that the LORD was with him and that the LORD made all he did to prosper in his hand. 4 So Joseph found favor in his sight, and served him. Then he made him overseer of his house, and all that he had he put in his hand. 5. . . the LORD blessed the Egyptians house for Josephs sake Also 21-23.

Deuteronomy 28: 1-13

1 ... If you diligently obey the voice of the LORD your God, to observe carefully all His commandments...that the LORD your God will set you high above all nations of the earth: 2 And all these blessings shall come upon you (Verses 3-13 describe the blessings promised) Also 30:1,2,9,10,15,16.

Joshua 1:8

This Book of the Law shall not depart from your mouth, but you shall meditate in it day and night, that you may observe to do according to all that is written in it. For then you will make your way prosperous, and then you will have good success.

Psalm 1:1-3

1 Blessed is the man who walks not in the counsel of the ungodly. .. 2 But his delight is in the law of the LORD, And in His law he meditates day and night. 3 He shall be like a tree
planted by the rivers of water, That brings forth its fruit in its season, whose leaf also shall not wither; And whatever he does shall prosper.

Psalm 73

Here Asaph tells how he was envious of the wicked in their seeming prosperity (v. 2-16) until he saw how slippery was their hold (17-22); then he saw the blessings of the righteous (23-28) true prosperity! Also Psalm 37:34-40.

Philippians 4: 19
God promises through the Apostle Paul that, since the Philippi church has given so generously to him in the Lord's work, God will supply all their need.

n. GIVING TO GOD AND TO PEOPLE

1. The tithe is God's minimum, taught by the Law, by practice, and by New Testament approval.

Genesis 14:20
Before the Law was given, Abraham gave tithes of all that he gained in battle. He gave them to Melchizedek, recognizing him as a representative of God.

Genesis 28:22
Jacob too promised a tenth to God at Bethel.

Leviticus 27:30-34
The details of the tithe for Israel are given here: 30 And all the tithe of the land, whether of the seed of the land or of the fruit of the tree, is the Lords. It is holy to the LORD.

Numbers 18:24-29
24 For the tithes of the children of Israel...I have given to the Levites as an inheritance; therefore I have said to them, 'Among the children of Israel they shall have no inheritance.' 26 Speak thus to the Levites, ... When you take from the children of Israel the tithes which I have given you from them as your inheritance, then you shall offer up...to the LORD, a tenth of the tithe. Also Deuteronomy 12:6,7; Malachi 3:8-10.

2 Chronicles 31:5-14
When Hezekiah initiated the keeping of the Passover once again, and with it other reforms, he commanded that once again the people should bring in their tithes and offerings. They did so abundantly. 5 As soon as the commandment was circulated, the children of Israel brought in abundance the first fruits of grain and wine, oil and honey, and of all the produce of the field; and they brought in abundantly the tithe on everything.

Matthew 23:23
Jesus condemns the Pharisees as hypocrites, saying that though they tithed, they were not consistent in their actions in other manners of the law which were even more crucial. 23... These [other responsibilities] you ought to have done, without leaving the others [the tithe] undone.
Here is His approval of the tithe.

Hebrews 7:4-10
In the discussion here concerning Abraham's giving of the tithe to Melchizedek, the importance of the tithe as a recognition of one who is greater and to be honored is recognized.

2. God blesses those who are generous with Him.

Proverbs 3:9,10
9 Honor the LORD with your possessions, and with the first fruits of all your increase: 10 So your barns will be filled with plenty, and your vats will overflow with new wine.

Proverbs 11 :24,25
24 There is one who scatters, yet increases more; and there is one who withholds more than is right, but it leads to poverty. 25 The generous soul will be made rich, and he who waters will also be watered himself.

Malachi 3:8-10
10 Bring all the tithes. . . and prove me.. . if I will not open you the windows of heaven, and pour you out a blessing.

Matthew 6:31-34
33 But seek first the kingdom of God and His righteousness, and all these things shall be added to you. Also Deuteronomy 28:11,12; 30:9,10.

Matthew 26:7-13
Lavish giving to the Lord is not wasted. The precious ointment was an act of worship from one who loved Him.

Mark 10:29,30
29 No one who has left house or brothers...for my sake. .. 30 But he shall receive a hundredfold. (1OOxs)

Mark 12:41-44
Jesus commended the widow for giving all she had into the treasury. Also Luke 21 :3,4.

Luke 6:38
Give and it shall be given to you...for with the same measure. . . it will be measured back to you.

2 Corinthians 9:6-12
He who sows bountifully will also reap bountifully... God loves a cheerful giver.

Philippians 4: 14-19
15 No church shared with me concerning giving and receiving but you only... 16 You sent aid once and again   19 And my God shall supply all your need...

3. Giving to God should be in proportion to the way God has prospered us.

Deuteronomy 16: 17
   Every man shall give as he is able, <u>according</u> to the blessing of the LORD your God which He has given you.

Ezra 2:68,69
   68 Some of the heads of the fathers' houses, when they came to the house of the LORD... the house of the LORD which is in Jerusalem, offered freely for the house of God... 69 According to their <u>ability,</u> they gave to the treasury. ...

Malachi 3:8
   Will a man rob God? Yet you have robbed Me! But you say, 'In what way have we robbed You?'In tithes and offerings.

Mark 12:41-44
   The significance of the gift given by the poor widow was based on her attitude and the proportion of her gift to her total assets, not on the amount itself.

1 Corinthians 16:2
   On the first day of the <u>week</u> let each one of you lay something aside, storing up as he may prosper

2 Corinthians 8: 12
   For if there is first a willing mind, it is accepted according to what one has, and not according to what he does not have.

NOTE: "I never knew a child of God being bankrupted by his benevolence. What we keep we may lose, but what we give to Christ we are sure to keep. "
- Theodore L. Cuyler, 1822-1909.

4. Giving to the Lord should be a private matter based on one's own decisions.

Exodus 25:1,2
   2 Speak to the children of Israel, that they bring Me an offering. From everyone who gives it willingly with his heart you shall take My offering. Also 35:5.

Exodus 35:21-29
   Then everyone came whose heart was stirred, and everyone whose spirit was willing, and they brought the Lords offering for the work of the tabernacle... (v. 21). A description of the abundance offered so willingly follows in the next verses.

Ezra 2:68,69
   68 Some of the fathers... offered freely... 69 According to their ability

Matthew 6: 1-4

1 Take heed that you do not do your charitable deeds before men, to be seen by them 3 ... Do not let your left hand know what your right hand is doing, 4 that your charitable deed may be in secret

Acts 5:1-5

Peter reminds Ananias that after his land was sold, the money was his to control. He need not have given all or part of it, but what he gave should be done willingly and honestly.

2 Corinthians 8:1-5

In giving to the poor saints at Jerusalem, the Macedonian churches were freely willing, imploring us with much urgency that we would receive the gift. . . (v. 3, 4).

2 Corinthians 9:7

So Let each one give as he purposes in his heart, not grudgingly or of necessity; for God loves a cheerful giver.

5. God considers our giving an investment: He keeps accounts.

Mathew 6:20,21

20 But lay up for yourselves treasures in heaven, where neither moth nor rust destroys and where thieves do not break in and steal. 21 For where your treasure is, there your heart will be also.

Matthew 19:27-30

God promises reward to those who make sacrifices on earth. 29 And everyone who has left houses or brothers or sisters or father or mother or wife or children or lands, for My names sake, shall receive a hundredfold, and inherit everlasting life. [Alan D. Dickinson].

Philippians 4: 17

Paul, commending the Philippians for their gifts: Not that I seek the gift, but I seek the fruit that abounds to your account.

6. Offerings to God should be honestly and fairly handled.

Exodus 22:29,30

Offerings should not be delayed, but given promptly.

Deuteronomy 23: 18

Offering money should be that which is gained honestly and honorably. Also 2 Sam. 24:24.

2 Corinthians 8: 18-22

Proper precautions should be taken that the money given is administered properly. Also 1 Cor. 16:2,3.

7. Those who serve the Lord full-time should also give of their substance to the Lord.

Numbers 18:26-32
    The Levites were to tithe the offerings that were given to them, giving the best to God

    "There Is no portion of money that Is our money, and the rest Gods money. It Is all His; He made It all, gives it all, and He has simply trusted It to us for His service. A servant has two purses, the masters and his own, but we have only one. "
- Adolphe Monod.

8. God expects both individuals and churches to be generous with those in need.

Deuteronomy 15:7-11
    7 If there Is among you a poor man of your brethren. "8 but you shall open your hand wide to him... 10 You shall surely give to him..for this thing the LORD your God will bless you Also Lev. 19:9,10,33,34; 23:22; 25:35-38.

Psalm 41:1
    Blessed is he who considers the poor; The LORD will deliver him in time of trouble. Also Prov 28:27.

Proverbs 19: 17
    He who has pity on the poor lends to the LORD, and He will pay back what he has given. Also 22:9.

Matthew 5:42
    Give to him who asks you, and from him who wants to borrow from you do not turn away.

Matthew 25:40
    Inasmuch as you did it to one of the least of these My brethren, you did it to Me. (Jesus).

Acts 20:35
    . By laboring like this, that you must support the weak. And remember the words of the Lord Jesus, that He said, "It is more blessed to give than to receive."

2 Corinthians 8:1-5
    The example of the Macedonian churches who out of poverty gave beyond their power, after they first gave their own selves to the Lord. Also 12-15.

Ephesians 4:28
    Let him labor, working with his hands what is good, that he may have something to give him who has need! A somewhat surprising reason for working!

1 Timothy 6: 17-19
    17 Command those who are rich... 18 that they be rich in good works, ready to give, willing to share. Also Heb. 13: 16.

1 John 3:17
    But whoever has this worlds goods, and sees his brother in need, and shuts up his heart from him, how does the love of God abide in him?

    "Riches without charity are nothing worth. They are a blessing only to him who makes them a blessing to others. "
- Henry Fielding, 1707-1754.

    "Serving God with our little, is the way to make it more; and we must never think that wasted with which God is honored, or men are blest. "
-John Hall, 1829-1898.

9. God's way of providing for needs is through the "gifts" of His people.

Exodus 25:1-9
    The people were instructed to bring materials for the tabernacle building - i.e., specified items. Also 35:21-29, the people willingly gave; in 36:5-7, more than enough was given.

Numbers 7: 1-8
    The twelve princes who had been in charge of taking the census brought as gifts for the Lord six covered wagons and twelve oxen. This was God's way of providing for   the transporting of the tabernacle and the court - i.e., boards, sockets, bars, hangings, et cetera.

Deuteronomy 18: 1 - 5
    1 The priests, the Levites...shall have no part nor inheritance with Israel: they shall eat the offerings of the Lord... In other words it was the offerings of others that were to provide for these needs.

Ezra 1 :4-6; 2:68,69
    The method of voluntary gifts for a particular need was recognized even by a heathen king, Cyrus, when he made proclamation concerning Jews retuning to Jerusalem to build a temple. 4 And whoever remains in any place where he sojourns, let the men of his place help him with silver and gold, with goods and livestock, besides the freewill offerings for the house of God which is in Jerusalem.

2 Corinthians 8: 13, 14
    13 For I do not mean that others should be eased and you burdened: 14 But by an equality... your abundance may supply their lack...

James 2:15,16

15 If a brother or sister is naked, and destitute of daily food, 16 and one of you says to them, Depart in peace. . . but you do not give them the things which are needed for the body, what does it profit?

III. FINANCIAL MANERS AND MEN'S RELATIONSHIPS

1. Those who are sent out by God to serve Him can expect Him to supply their material ($) needs.

Leviticus 2:3,10

A major portion of certain offerings in the tabernacle was to go to Aaron and his sons, or to the priest who offered it. Also 6:16,17,26; 7:6-15; 22:10-13.

Numbers 18:21,24,31

The Levites received the tithes of Israel. They also received towns and pasture lands. Also 35: 1-8 and Deut. 14:27.

Matthew 10:7-12

Jesus sent out the twelve without provision, expecting their needs to be supplied as they went. Also Luke 9:3-5.

Luke 10:1-11

Jesus sent out the seventy without purse or extra clothing, expecting them to be cared for as they went.

1 Corinthians 9 :6-16

Paul shows the reasonableness of support at the hands of others - the soldier, the farmer, the cattle-raiser, the ox that treads the grain, those who minister in the Jewish temple. The climax in
v. 14: Even so the Lord has commanded that those who preach the gospel should live from the gospel.

2. God, in some cases, directs a believer to support himself in doing the Lord's work.

Acts 20:33,34

Paul: 33 I have coveted no mans silver, or gold, or apparel. 34 Yes, you yourselves know that these hands have provided for my necessities, and for those who were with me. Also v. 35.

1 Corinthians 9: 14, 15

14 Even so the Lord has commanded that those who preach the gospel should live from the gospel. 15 But I have used none of these things, nor have I written these things that it should be done so to me, " Also 2 Cor. 11:7-12.

1 Thessalonians 2:9

For you remember, brethren, our labor and toil; for laboring night and day, that we might not be a burden to any of you, we preached to you the gospel of God.

3. That which is valuable must sometimes be destroyed because of the danger of its leading into sin.

Deuteronomy 7:25

As Israel captured villages, they were to destroy utterly the graven images, not even saving the silver and gold, 25 Lest you be snared by it. They were expressly told not to bring an image into the house 26 Lest you be doomed to destruction like it (v. 26). Also 13:16,17.

Deuteronomy 20: 16-18

16 But of the cities of these peoples which the LORD your God gives you as an inheritance, you shall let nothing that breathes remain alive: 17 But you shall utterly destroy them:... just as the LORD your God has commanded you: 18 Lest they teach you to do according to all their abominations which they have done for their gods, and you sin against the LORD your Cod.

Mathew 18:8,9

The same principle reiterated by the Lord Jesus: 8 And if your hand or foot causes you to sin, cut It off and cast it from you. It is better for you to enter into life lame or maimed, rather than having two hands or two feet, to be cast into the everlasting fire.

4. Believers should not expect unbelievers to understand or follow Biblical standards in handling money or possessions. [However often they dol.

Genesis 14:22-24

Though Abraham refused to take goods offered by the king of Sodom lest that heathen king declare, / have made Abraham rich, he let his confederates take their portion (v. 13,24).

Genesis 23: 7-16

Abraham insisted on paying for the field and cave of Machpelah as a burying place for his family, even though Ephron the Hittite was insistent that he accept it without payment.

5. Believers may rightfully give special consideration to other believers.

Deuteronomy 15: 1-3

In giving the law concerning the sabbatical year, God directed that Israelites make a difference in their handling of loans made to fellow Jews and those made to foreigners. 2... Every creditor who has lent anything to his neighbor shall release it; he shall not require it of his neighbor or his brother, because it is called the Lords release. 3 Of a foreigner you may require it; but your hand shall release what is owed by your brother.

Deuteronomy 23: 19.20
The law in Israel: 19 You shall not charge interest to your brother-interest on money or food or anything that is lent out at interest: 20 To a foreigner you may charge interest, but to your brother you shall not charge interest, that the LORD your God may bless you...

Galatians 6: 10
Therefore, as we have opportunity, let us do good to all, especially to those who are of the household of faith.

6. Believers are Not to base their respect for people on their wealth.

James 2:1-9
God's condemnation for basing respect on the amount of one's possessions is summarized in v. 9: But f you show partiality, you commit sin, and are convicted by the law   as transgressors. In addition, other logical reasons for not giving favored treatment to wealthy persons are given: (1) by doing so, one makes himself a judge of the thought life of another (v. 2-4); (2) God has shown special concern for the poor, in making many of them rich in faith (v. 5, 6); (3) the rich more than the poor often blaspheme God and oppress believers (v. 6, 7); (4) God's law is summed up in loving of one's neighbor, whether rich or poor (v. 8,9).

7. Lending and borrowing money are connected with freedom for a nation 'or' a person.

Deuteronomy 15:6
Spoken to Israel: For the LORD your God will bless you just as He promised you; you shall lend to many nations, but you shall not borrow; you shall reign over many nations, but they shall not reign over you. Also 28:12,13.

Proverbs 22:7
The rich rules over the poor, and the borrower is servant to the lender.

IV. PROPERTY OWNERSHIP

1. Property rights are to be protected.

Exodus 20: 15, 17
75 You shall not steal... 17 You shall not covet... Also Lev. 19: 11,13; Provo 28:24.

Exodus 21:33-36
Negligence that causes loss to another person must be paid for; it is also considered sin. Also 22:5-15; Lev. 6:1-7.

Exodus 22: 1-15
Such actions as stealing, burglarizing, permitting a straying animal to damage property, not giving proper protection to money or goods left in one's care and borrowing an animal and letting it die demand restitution.

Leviticus 24: 18,21
One who kills a beast must make good to its owner.

Deuteronomy 22: 1-3
Lost property or straying animals are to be returned.

Deuteronomy 23:24,25
A person was permitted to eat grapes or com from his neighbor's crop, but not to harvest and take home any.

Joshua 13-19
Each tribe of Israel was to own certain land, according as the Lord commanded Moses to divide it (14:5). Also Ezekiel 47:13,14.

1 Kings 21: 17-19
Elijah was sent by God to reprimand King Ahab for killing Naboth in order to take possession of his vineyard.

Proverbs 22:28
Markers designating property boundaries were not to be removed. Also 23: 10, 11; Deut. 19: 14.

Ezekiel 46: 18
God forbids a ruler from confiscating property to provide an inheritance for his sons.

Ezekiel 47:22,23
God makes clear His concern for Gentiles as well as Jews. Here He gives direction concerning the dividing of the land, but specifically commands that strangers that sojourn among you, and who bear children among you shall be included in the inheritance, in the tribes in which they live.

2. An owner has a right to buy, sell, or otherwise dispose of his own property.

Proverbs 31:16,24
A woman, described as buying a field, planting a vineyard, making fine linen, selling it, and delivering girdles unto the merchant, is called virtuous.

Mathew 20: 1-] 6
Parable of the man who paid the same wage for different hours of work. 15 Is it not lawful for me to do what 1 wish with my own things?

Acts 5:3,4
Peter reminded Ananias concerning the sale of his property: While it remained, was it not your own? And after it was sold, was it not in your own control?

3. The right to privacy in one's home, or freedom from unlawful search, is a God-given right [and a U.S. Constitutional Right as well].

Deuteronomy 24: 10,11
    Under God's law, a man who lent money to a fellow-citizen, with the loan guaranteed by a pledge of some sort, had no right to enter the house of the borrower to search out the article pledged. He must wait for the owner to bring the article out to him.

NOTE: "Property is very dear to men... because it is the bulwark of all they hold dearest on earth, and above all else, because it is the safeguard of those they love. "
- William G Sumner, 1840-1910.

4. Property ownership is to pass from one generation to another.

Numbers 27:8-11
    In Israel under the Law, when a man died his property was to go to his sons, daughters, or nearest relatives.

Numbers 36
    Each tribe's inheritance was to remain the property of that tribe; this regulation was so important that freedom to marry outside the tribe had to be forfeited to carry it out.

Deuteronomy 21: 15-17
    Property rights of the first born were to be protected in case a man later had sons by a second wife.

Ezekiel 46: 16-18
    Even in the future, property is to be kept within the families of Israel's princes.

5. Though voluntary communal ownership has Scriptural precedent for believers, it must be done honestly and out of love for one another: the fact that such ownership created problems and is "never" recommended in the Epistles is doubtless significant.

Acts 2:44,45
    44 Now all who believed were together, and had all things in common; 45 and sold their possessions and goods, and divided them among all, as anyone had need. Also 4:32-37.

Acts 5: 1-11
    The dishonesty of Ananias and Sapphira, and God's judgment of them.

6. "Women" as well as men have property rights.

Numbers 27:1-9 Cf. Job 42:15
    God approved the request of the daughters of Zelophehad for an inheritance in Israel, since they did not have brothers (v. 8). Also 36:5-12; Joshua, 17:3, 4.

Proverbs 31:16,18,24

A virtuous woman considers a field and buy it; she knows her merchandise is good; she makes fine linen and sells it along with finished garments.

Acts 5:7-10

Sapphira, as well as Ananias, was considered responsible for the disposition of their property; she too was judged for the dishonesty.

7. One who invests money has a right to a return on his investment, "providing" that return is not gained by taking advantage of the poor.

Exodus 22:25

If you lend money to any of My people who are poor among you, you shall not be like a moneylender to him; you shall not charge him interest.

Deuteronomy 24:6

No man shall take the lower or the upper millstone in pledge, for he takes ones living in pledge. The millstones were essential for meal preparation.

Proverbs 28:8

One who increases his possessions by usury and extortion gathers it for him who will pity the poor.

Mathew 25:15-30

The parable of the talents. The condemnation of the man who did not invest his money for gain is expressed in v. 27, 28: 27 Therefore you ought to have deposited my money with the bankers, and at my coming 1 would have received back my own with interest. 28 Therefore take the talent from him, and give it to him who has ten talents... 30 And cast the   unprofitable servant into the outer darkness... The application which the Lord makes here indicates approval, or at least recognition of the legitimacy of gain.

Luke 19:11-25

The parable of the ten pounds. 23 Why then did you not put my money in the bank, that at my coming 1 might have collected it with interest? Here also the application is similar. Also Mark 12: 1-9.

V. PROBLEMS RELATED TO MONEY AND PROPERTY

1. The love of material things leads to Tall kinds and types of problems.

Proverbs 15:27 - trouble in the home

He who is greedy for gain, troubles his own house .

Proverbs 22: 16 - poverty

He who oppresses the poor to increase his riches, and he who gives to the rich, will surely come to poverty.

Proverbs 28:20-22 - sin, poverty

20. . . but he who hastens to be rich will not go unpunished. 22 A man with an evil eye hastens after riches, and does not consider that poverty will come upon him.

Ecclesiastes 5: 1 0-16 - lack of anticipated satisfaction

10 He who loves silver will not be satisfied with silver; nor he who loves abundance, with increase. This also is vanity. 11 When goods increase, they increase who eat them; So what
profit have the owners except to see them with their eyes? 13 There is a severe evil which I have seen under the sun: riches kept for their owner to his hurt. Surely King Solomon was well
acquainted with the results of a lust for riches!

Isaiah 56:9-12 - selfishness, blindness to real issues and drunkenness

God describing Israel: 9 ...beasts... come to devour...10 ...watchmen are blind... all ignorant¬ dumb dogs, they cannot bark; sleeping, lying down, loving to slumber... 11 ...greedy dogs which never have enough... shepherds who cannot understand: they all look to their own way, every one for his gain, from his own territory 12 ...we will ill ourselves with intoxicating drink. .. See also Ezekiel 22:12,13,25-29.

Matthew 13:22 - choking of the Word and unfruitfulness

Now he who received seed among the thorns is he who hears the word, and the cares of this world and the deceitfulness of riches choke the word, and he becomes unfruitful.

Matthew 19:21-24; Mark 10:21-25 - forfeiting [losing] eternal life

21 Jesus said to him, ...Sell what you have and give to the poor, and you will have treasure in heaven... 22 But when the young man heard that saying, he went away sorrowful, for he had great possessions. [He was very, very rich].

Luke 12: 13-34 - an empty life of worry and being overly anxious

The parable of the rich man who built bigger and better barns, but failed to seek after God.

1 Timothy 6: 9, 10 - temptation, lusts and all kinds of major evil

9 But those who desire to be rich fall into temptation and a snare, and into many foolish and harmful lusts which drown men in destruction and perdition. 10 For the love of money is a root of all kinds of evil...

James 4: 1- 3 - lust, wars and fighting

1 Where do wars and fights come from among you? Do they not come from your desires for pleasure that war in your members? Also 5:1-6; 1 John 2:15,16.

2. Just wealth and prosperity themselves can lead to problems.

Deuteronomy 8: 11-18 - forgetting the Lord; taking undue credit

God warns Israel before they enter the Land: 11 Beware that you do not forget the LORD your Cod... 12 Lest-when you have eaten and are full, and have built beautiful houses and dwell in them; 13 and when your herds and your locks multiply, and your silver and your sold are multiplied, and all that you have is multiplied; 14 when your heart is lifted up, and you forget the LORD your God who brought you out of the land of Egypt. " 15 Who led you... 16 Who fed you... 17 then you say in your heart, "My power and the might of my hand have gained me this wealth."

Proverbs 19:6 - false fiends [be very careful].

Many entreat the favor of the nobility, and every man is a friend to one who gives gifts.

Ecclesiastes 5: 1 0-16 - a whole variety of problems

Solomon, out of his personal experience with great riches, is used by the Lord to issue some awnings concerning the problems wealth may bring: he cites covetousness, expense, worry, sickness, lack of joy, insomnia, losses, lack of permanence after this life [Heaven].   Also Proverbs 20:21.

1 Timothy 6: 17 -19 - pride, trust in wealth and hoarding

A waning to New Testament believers about special dangers to those who were rich in the things of this world.

3. Poverty may result from several causes about which God "warns" us.

Proverbs 11:24 - hoarding

...There is one who withholds more than is right, but it leads to poverty.

Proverbs 13:18 - refusing instruction

Poverty and shame will come to him who disdains correction, but he who regards reproof will be honored.

Proverbs 14:23 - talking too much

...Idle chatter leads only to poverty.

Proverbs 20:13 - laziness

Do not love sleep, lest you come to poverty; open your eyes, and you will be satisfied with bread.

Proverbs 22:16 - taking advantage of the poor; catering to the rich

He who oppresses the poor to increase his riches, and he who gives to the rich, will surely come to poverty.

Proverbs 23:20, 21 - drunkenness, overeating and oversleeping

20 Do not mix with winebibbers, or with gluttonous eaters of meat: 21 For the drunkard and the glutton will come to poverty, and drowsiness will clothe a man with rags.

Proverbs 28:19, 22 - bad fiends and being in a hurry to become rich
19. . .He who follows frivolity will have poverty enough! 20 he who hastens to be rich... 22 consider that poverty will come upon him. Also v. 20.

Jeremiah 17:11 - getting riches by the wrong methods
...He who gets riches, but not by right; it will leave him in the midst of his days, and at his end he will be a fool.

Isaiah 65:12, 13 - refusing to hear and obey God
12 ...When I called, you did not answer; when I spoke, you did not hear, but did evil before My eyes, and chose that in which I do not delight. 13 Therefore thus says the Lord God:
"Behold, My servants shall eat, but you shall be hungry...shall drink, but you shall be thirsty:... shall rejoice, but you shall be ashamed.

4. One who is security for another's debts is courting trouble.

Proverbs 6: 1- 5
/ My son, if you become surety for your friend, if you have shaken hands in pledge for a stranger, 2 you are snared by the words of your own mouth; you are taken by the word, of your mouth. The following verses urge immediate extracting of oneself from the agreement, before sleeping!

Proverbs 11: 15
He who is surety for a stranger will suffer for it, but one who hates being surety is secure.

Proverbs 17:18
A man devoid of understanding shakes hands in a pledge, and becomes surety for his friend.

Proverbs 22:26,27
26 Do not be one of those who shakes hands in a pledge, one of those who is surety for debts. 21 If you have nothing with which to pay, why should he take away your bed from under you?

THE REAL OFFERING GOD WANTS

God wanted offerings in 'old' testament times, but he wanted the people to bring them because they loved Him and were trying to live the best lives they could. God was not pleased with offerings of animals from people who kept doing wicked things most of the time.

Today, 'NEW' testament times, God wants us to give a certain portion (varies with each individual) of our income (net or gross this also varies with each individual) because we love Him, out of hearts of praise, and because are trying to live holy and un sinful lives (of course we all still sin on occasion).

"Who has ever given to God, that He should repay them? For from God and through Him and to Him are <u>ALL</u> things..." (including money) Romans 11:35

<u>BIBLE REFERENCES</u>

Gen, 43:12 ...take back the money in your hand.
Eccles. 5:10 ...they who <u>love</u> money, will not be satisfied. Eccles. 7:12 ...
Eccles. 10:19 ...money is the answer to (Foolishness). Matt. 21:2...
Mark 6:8...
Luke 19:23 ...
I Tim. 3:3 ...be free from the <u>love</u> of money.
1 Tim. 6:10 ...the <u>love</u> of money is the root of all kinds of evil.
2 Kings 5:26 ...
Jer. 32:25 ...
Amos 2:6 ...

<u>WHEN YOU NEED FINANCES</u>

But remember the Lord your God, for it is he who gives you the ability to produce wealth, and so confirms his covenant, which he Swore to your forefathers, as it is today.

Deuteronomy 8:18

For the Lord your God will bless you as he has promised, and you will lend to many nations but will borrow from none. You will rule over many nations but none will rule over you.

Deuteronomy 15:6

The Lord will open the heavens, the storehouse of his bounty, to send rain on your land in season and to bless all the work of your hands. You will lend to many nations but will borrow from none.

Deuteronomy 28: 12

If they obey and serve him, they will spend the rest of their days in prosperity and their years in contentment.

Job 36:11

I know that there is nothing better for men than to be happy and do good while they live. That everyone may eat and drink, and find satisfaction in all his toil - this is the gift of God.

Ecclesiastes 3: 12,13

The thief comes only to steal and kill and destroy; I have come that they may have life, and have it to the full.

John 10:10

Each man should give what he has decided in his heart to give, not reluctantly or under compulsion, for God loves a cheerful giver. And God is able to make all grace abound to you, so that in all things at all times, having all that you need, you will abound in every good work.

2 Corinthians 9:7,8

Do not store up for yourselves treasures on earth, where moth and rust destroy, and where thieves break in and steal. But store up for yourselves treasures in heaven, where moth and rust do not destroy, and where thieves do not break in and steal. For where your treasure is, there your <u>heart</u> will be also.

Matthew 6:19-21

A faithful man will be richly blessed, but one eager to get rich quick will not go unpunished.

Proverbs 28:20

Command those who are rich in this present world not to be arrogant nor to put their hope in wealth, which is so uncertain, but to put their hope in God, who richly provides us with everything for our enjoyment. Command them to do good, to be rich in good deeds, and to be generous and willing to share. In this way they will lay up treasure for themselves as a firm foundation for the coming age, so that they may take hold of the life that is truly life.

1 Timothy 6: 17-19

Will a man rob God? Yet you rob me. But you ask, "How do we rob you?" "In tithes and offerings. "You are under a curse - the whole nation of you - because you are robbing me. "Bring the whole tithe into the storehouse, that there may be food in my house. Test me in this," says the Lord Almighty, "and see if I will not throw open the floodgate of heaven <u>and</u> pour out so much blessing that you will not have room enough for it."

Malachi 3:8-10

Not that I am looking for a gift, but I am looking for what may be credited to <u>your</u> account. I have received full payment and even more; I am amply supplied, now that I have received from Epaphroditus the gifts you sent. They are a fragrant offering, an acceptable   sacrifice, pleasing to God. And my God will meet ALL your needs according to his glorious riches in Christ Jesus.

Philippians 4:17-19

Give, and it will be given to you. A good measure, pressed down, shaken together and running over, will be poured into <u>your</u> lap. For with the measure you use, it will be measured to you.

Luke 6:38

Remember this: Whoever sows sparingly will also reap sparingly, <u>and</u> whoever sows generously will also reap generously. One man gives freely, yet gains even more; another withholds unduly, but comes to poverty.

Proverbs 11:24

MONEY CHANGER'S - MONEY LENDER'S

(Creditor) (For more information on money changers, please see the Moneychanger: Autobiography by said author)

Luke 7:41

FINANCIAL WORSHIP

Giving to the work of God.
Everything we have is from God (Deut. 8:17, 18). Our financial life is just another area of our life in which we need to put God first. In the Old Testament putting God first was done with the tithe (giving 10% to God.) (Lev. 27:32; Prov. 3:9, 10; Mai. 3:10) The tithe was not restated in the New Testament as a law. Jesus challenged His followers to live by a higher standard than the legalistic righteousness of the Old Testament. (Mt. 5:20). The New Testament principles are to put the Lord first in your life and give as you are prospered. On the first day of the week,
each one of you should set aside a sum (varies with individual) of money in keeping with his income... I Cor. 16:2.

From I Cor. 16;2 we learn:
• Regular giving - "on the first day of the week."
• Personal giving - "each one of you" - God wants every member to give responsibly.
• Planned giving - "set aside a sum of money" - not an afterthought.
• Proportionate giving - "in keeping with his income." As you consider what you should give, ask yourself:
• Have I prayed about what the Lord would have me give?
• Will this amount motivate me to greater faithfulness?
• Does my giving reflect my desire to see the Kingdom of God grow?

MONEY ($) QUESTIONS

1) Is it better to give than to receive? or, 2) Is it better to receive than to give (vice versa)? These are two age old questions, right? More so in the secular earthly (Human) world than in the Christian world, I must add.

CHAPTER VI

CHAPTER VI
Myths About Money

I personally have several strong opinions (myths?) about money ($) and I (this said author) will share some of them later in this chapter:

Money Myths

Money myths are global beliefs about all the wonderful, almost __magical__ things that money can do for us. Though each of these myths contains some modicum of truth, taking them as __gospel__ can prevent us from making rational decisions with our money. Here's how to identify and debunk some of the myths that may be causing problems in your   financial   as   well   as   your personal life.

Most North Americans believe in at least one money myth; many of us believe in a number of them. These beliefs can trigger intense emotions about money (anxiety, fear, obsession) and can even make it difficult for us to handle the simplest financial decisions and   tasks.
Here are the six (6) most common money myths:
   Money = Happiness
   Money = Freedom
   Money = Love
   Money = Self-worth
   Money   =   Power
   Money = Security
What do we need to do about these money myths? First we must identify the myths that are affecting us personally. Next we must spend some time debunking the money myths, one by one. Only then will we be free to use money and make decisions about our money in a way that enhances our life rather than constrains it.

MONEY = HAPPINESS

Money equals happiness is one of the most prevalent myths in our culture. We are raised on stories about people who worked hard, struck it rich and lived happily ever after.   Such individuals as Andrew Carnegie, Oprah Winfrey, Ted Turner, Jane Fonda, and Bill Gates serve as the quintessential models of success. But do we really know enough about these men and women to know if they are truly happy and whether money is the primary factor in   their supposed happiness?

Even our old tired jokes reflect this pervasive belief that money equals happiness. Consider these common sayings: "Being rich isn't everything, but it sure beats whatever is in second place!" and "I've been rich and I've been poor, and rich is better."

Of course, being poor or financially stressed definitely does affect our happiness. But it is not the __prime__ determinant of our happiness and satisfaction in life, and we would do well to remember this. Otherwise, we will be divan to amass large sums of money in a way that may well impinge on or even destroy the happiness we hoped money would create.

M Do you believe that Money = Happiness?

If you want to know for sure whether you believe in the money-is-happiness myth, ask yourself the following questions:

• Do you catch yourself thinking, "If only I had (made) a little more money (or a lot more money), everything would be great"?

• Do you envy others who make more money than you do, or who have more money or more things, assuming that they must be happier than you are because of their greater financial ease?

• When you encounter someone who you know is not very wealthy, do you assume that the person couldn't really be happy?

• Would having to take a small decrease in your own or your partner's income make you feel very upset?

If you answered yes to at least three of these five questions, you're influenced by the money-equals-happiness myth. [Maybe a little bit to me - Author.]

M Debunking Money = Happiness

To begin to challenge this belief, I recommend that you think about, write down, or tape-record the answers to the following questions:

• What two activities do you love to do that make you happy?

• How much does it cost to do these activities?

• Are these activities best done alone or with others?

I have done this exercise with many diverse groups through the years. Invariably, the majority of people in each group will choose at least one activity that costs very little money or no money at all. (For most people, _making love_ is on the first list!) And most people find that at least one of their activities, if not both, is best done with another person. So maybe it is social connections that equals happiness? Participants in my workshops are pleasantly surprised when they realize that many of the things they love in their lives cost nothing or next to nothing. If your results are similar, let this awareness remind you that much of your happiness has very little to do with money.

Here's another useful exercise to try:

• For one week or one month, keep track of what you spend your money on.

• On a scale of 1 to 10, rate the fulfillment that each expenditure brings you.

This exercise can be a real eye-opener, for it shows you many ways in which you use your money that don't add one iota to your happiness and fulfillment.

If, after reading and trying these exercises, you still believe that "if only I had more money, I'd really be happy," take a little time to search for and note examples that run counter to the money-equals-happiness myth. Think about people you know personally, or have read or heard about, who:

• Don't have a lot of money but are very happy, or

• Have a lot of money and are not happy.

When I was a guest on a TV talk show in 1991,1 met Dennis, an earnest man who had just won the lottery. He shared with me his feelings of unhappiness and anxiety after this supposedly wonderful event brought him a large amount of money. Dennis had had dozens of business proposals - and even a few marriage proposals from women he didn't know! He had become mistrustful: how could he possibly distinguish between those who were reacting to his money and those who were responding to him as an individual? This windfall   made   Dennis's life a living hell for a while. And even though he was leaning how to deal with his situation, he would never say that for him, money equaled happiness. In fact, many other lottery winners also report that the vast change in their financial status has had a very destabilizing effect on their lives and has created more problems than it solved.

Here is a final assignment for those of you who feel affected or controlled by this money myth:

• Everyday for a week, spend time on activities, old or new, that cost little or nothing and that bring you happiness.

• Notice and record your feelings about each of these activities. Doing this assignment will help you realize that there is much in your life (or there could be) that costs little and makes you happy.

You may also be heartened by the testimony of readers of a magazine called "The Sun", who wrote in on the subject of wealth. It was startling to see how many of the letters did not equate real wealth - and the feeling of abundance that comes from deep fulfillment - with financial wealth. Many of their letters said, in essence, "When I think back on the past 20 years, I realize that my husband [or my wife] and I were happiest when we were making less money. Our lives were simpler; we were more creative about doing things we wanted to do; we were less workaholic; and we had more time and energy to enjoy life and each other. That seemed like true wealth to us."

In these recessionary times, with so much real financial <u>uncertainty</u> in the air, freeing yourself from the belief that money equals happiness can enable you to better roll with the punches. If you are denied a cost-of-living increase or a raise because of tough financial times at your job, you will tend to feel less depressed and deprived. Whatever the financial ups and downs, you'll stand a much better chance of getting enjoyment out of life.

MONEY = LOVE

Every time we turn on our TV, we are bombarded with commercials that try to link money with love in our minds. They tell us that if we would just buy this flower-fresh deodorant, or that new and improved shampoo, or the latest model of that snazzy spots car, we'd have all the love and happiness we could want. Advertisements in newspapers and magazines are sending us the same messages. This dangerous cultural conditioning, and the "keeping   up   with   the Joneses" mentality that fuels it, contributes to the epidemic of compulsive spending in this country. Many of us believe not only that money equals love but that money can substitute for a lack of love.

M Do you believe that Money = Love?

To find out if you are among the many who believe in the myth that money equals love, answer the following questions:

• When you feel lonely or depressed, do you buy yourself something to cheer yourself up?

• Do you tend to buy yourself something as a way of celebrating or rewarding yourself for a job well done?

• Do you tend to shop impulsively or compulsively?

• Do you buy things for yourself or others regardless of whether you have enough money to pay for these purchases?

• When you feel deprived or unloved, does buying yourself something seem like the first recourse?

If you answered yes to three or more of these questions, then money equals love for you, at least to some extent. [No, not to me.]

M Debunking Money = Love

If you subscribe to this myth in your actions and attitudes, you may need to spend some time thinking about people you know personally who:

• Don't have a lot of money but have a lot of love in their life.
• Have a lot of money but seem starved for love.

The next step in debunking this myth is to practice new ways of nurturing yourself that don't cost much money (or perhaps cost no money at all). If you tend to reward yourself by shopping (impulsively or compulsively), think of alternate activities that would serve the same purpose. For example, you might take a hot bath or have a long talk with your best friend. You could attend a religious service, listen to music, read a book, meditate, or go to a museum. The possibilities are endless!

If you feel that the urge to shop comes over you like a tidal wave, and that you can't say no to it, you may well have a spending addiction. There's no need to be ashamed about this problem; you are far from alone. Its source is usually a combination of early childhood deprivation (on an emotional, physical, or material level) as well as the social alienation that comes from being in a culture where there is a lack of community, a feeling of spiritual emptiness, and a craving to feel whole on some level. The only problem with the solution of using money as a substitute for love is that it doesn't work. It is like a Band-Aid on a festering wound, providing temporary relief from the feelings of loneliness, pain, or emptiness, but never actually healing the wound. In fact, these "quick fixes" erode self-esteem (self image)over time and create a self-perpetuating downward spiral that can often lead to more severe emotional as well as financial crises.

MONEY = POWER

The myth that money equals power is deeply entrenched in the media. Advertisements, especially car ads, are adept at communicating this (so-called) "truth." TV programs and movies show us rich men who control the world in exciting ways. They also demonstrate the flip-side of this myth: that money equals power in an evil sense, and that these rich people often end up destroying their lives or the lives of others with all their money.

As I said earlier, some truth is contained in every money myth. When we look around us, we see not just fictional but real-life examples of wealthy people who use their money and the status that may accompany it to wield power over others. It's been said that for many women, power is a great aphrodisiac; and wealthy men have often had an advantage in seducing and coupling with women. Many of us have had personal experience with superiors at work, who make more money and have more power than we do, using their authority over us in ways that constrain us and make us feel powerless. Having money can lead to more choices (of educational¬ and job training, for example) and can enable us to travel far and wide and to procure many of the things we want. It can buy good health care. And of course, all of these things are a kind of power.

But debunking the myth that money equals power can lead to new, creative life choices for us and our intimates.

M Do you believe that Money = Power?
To see if you believe in this money myth, ask yourself which of the following statements seem true to you:
• The most powerful people in the world are rich.
• If I had more money, I'd definitely be more powerful.
• When people lose money, they lose power.
• I need a lot of money to accomplish my goals and to feel in control of my life.
• Less money means less power to live my life as I choose.

If you agree with three or more of these statements, the money-equals-power myth seems at least partially true to you. (And also me.)

M Debunking Money = Power
If you think that money equals power in a positive sense (power to get what you want and need in life), then think about, write down, or tape- record your impressions of a few people you know personally, or have read or heard about, who:
• Don't have a lot of money but seem quite powerful.
• Have a lot of money but lack personal power.

Now consider:
• What factors (besides money) are necessary in attaining personal power (power to build a fulfilling life, accomplish life goals, maintain fulfilling relationships, etc.)?
• On a scale of 1 to 10, how would you rate the importance of money and these other factors in attaining these desired goals?

When I think of people who are not wealthy and have tremendous personal power, the first examples who come to mind are famous people who have changed the world in some sense. (For me, that is the height of personal power.) Mother Teresa (a true Saint), who took a vow of poverty and nurtured thousands of abandoned children; and Ralph Nader, who is famous for following a spat an lifestyle, has been working to make our society a better and safer place for consumers.

If you believe, on the other hand, that money equals power in a negative sense (power to corrupt and destroy lives), then you need to find examples of people you know personally, or have read or heard about, who:
• Have a lot of money and use it not to wield negative power but to enhance their lives and the lives of others.
• Don't have a lot of money but wield power in a negative way.

When I think about people who have a lot of money and use it well, I think about entertainers who sponsor benefits like live Aid, Comic Relief, and Farm Aid; Elizabeth Taylor and her work raising money to combat AIDS; and families such as the MacArthur's, who give grants to reward geniuses for their creative endeavors and to allow them to pursue their work less encumbered by financial constraints. I also think of Ben Cohen (of Ben and Jerry's ice cream), who organizes his business and uses his money to promote world peace, shared profit in business, and more egalitarian models of leadership. There are numerous other examples of people who use their wealth to enhance the lives of others.

But remember that money <u>cannot</u> buy personal fulfillment, and the power that comes from being truly in harmony with your own values and living out a life that you love and respect. Money cannot buy spiritual fulfillment; it cannot buy friendship. When we look around and see examples of those who thought they had tremendous financial power but then lost it - people like Leona Helmsley (Queen of Mean) and Ivan Boesky (Wall Street)- we realize that the heady wine of power through money may not ultimately be as satisfying as many of us think. It's not uncommon for people making huge amounts of money to be workaholics who sacrifice health and personal relationships for the power they think money will bring. So, in the end, what constitutes true power for us? Is it power over others, or control over our own lives? And aren't there many ways to achieve control over our own lives that are not determined by money?

Let's apply the idea of achieving personal power to your own life.
• In what areas of your life would you want to feel personally powerful?
• Is money involved in the attainment of all these goals, some of these goals, or none of these goals? If so, how much money?
• What adjectives would best describe how you would feel about achieving personal power in your own life?

MONEY = FREEDOM

Money equals freedom is a myth that many of us hold dear. As long as we secretly, or not so secretly, cling to this one, we never have to ask ourselves what we really want to do with our lives, and what might be preventing us from doing it. We can comfortably tell ourselves, "If only I had more money, I'd be free to paint; write that novel; travel to Europe; change professions... to do what I really want to do or what I was meant to do." And, of course, since doing some of the things we want to do in fact does cost money, the partial truth of this myth makes it convenient for us to hold on to it, instead of challenging the notion and perhaps
achieving real freedom.

M Do you believe that Money = Freedom?
If you think you may be controlled by this myth, determine whether you agree with the following statements:
• Having more money would enable me to do what I really want to do in my life. It is mainly money that is preventing me from doing what I really want to do.
• Wealthy people are truly freer to create the kind of life they want.
• The key to real freedom is to have enough money.
• I often think wistfully about all the things I could do, and all the freedom I would have, if only I had more money.

If you answered "true" to three or more of these statements, money equals freedom to you, at least to some degree. [Yes it does.]

M Debunking Money = Freedom
If you believe that money equals freedom, here's an exercise you can do to begin challenging this notion. Identify and describe, in as much detail as possible, a few people you   know
personally, or have read or heard about, who:
• Don't have a lot of money but seem very free to you.
• Have a lot of money but don't seem to be free at all.

Figuring out what constitutes true freedom is the work of a <u>lifetime</u>. But I don't believe that money is the major determinant - as long as we have enough to meet our basic needs and wants, for food, shelter, clothing, and for some pleasures of life that do cost money.

Speaking of pleasures, let's focus for a moment on travel. [I love to travel-Author.] Recently, a wise old friend of mine made some astute observations on the connection between money and the freedom to travel. He described the experiences of friends of his who had gone to Europe on a shoestring many years ago. They hitchhiked around, stayed in small villages as guests in the homes of people they met while traveling. They really got a sense of what each culture was like. He contrasted them to people he knew who were rich and wanted to go to Europe but who felt they had to stay home and make sure their money was growing. He also mentioned those who went to foreign counties and stayed in ritzy American-style hotels, never getting out and seeing the people and experiencing these cultures. To him, that didn't seem like freedom at all.

Of course, freedom is a <u>tricky</u> notion. We are not talking about freedom to act out all our impulses, however destructive. No amount of wealth makes this freedom permissible. We are talking about the freedom to do all that we wish to do, and to be all that we wish to be. [Be all that you can be.]

Let's now turn to an exercise that you might find useful in debunking the myth that money equals freedom:
• For one week (or one month), keep track of what you spend your money on.
• On a scale of 1 to 10, rate how much pleasure each expenditure brings you.
, • Note how much time you have to spend working to make the money to pay for these expenditures.

This process can be revealing, for it may point up ways that you are giving up your freedom and free time to purchase things you do not value or enjoy very much.

If you are willing to take a positive step in moving closer to your dreams and goals, think about the following:
• What could you do in the next six months that would give you more freedom without requiring a major change in your financial situation?
• What has prevented you from doing this thus far? Is it really money or something else?
• How could you do this, or take a step towards doing it, in the next week, couple of weeks, or month?

If you do take this action, remember to reward yourself and to monitor your thoughts and feelings (in writing, on tape, or at least in your mind) about moving in the direction of real freedom. [Be proud of yourself]

MONEY = SELF-WORTH

The myth of money equals self-worth comes up for many men and women when they're thinking about how much they're paid for the work they do. As a self-employed psy¬ chotherapist, I used to say to myself, "I'm trying to set a fee for my services, but how much am I worth?" My therapist colleagues in private practice are often heard asking themselves and one another the same question. Now it makes me cringe a little to realize how quickly we all equate our self-worth with the amount of money we charged for our work. Perhaps a more appropriate question to ask, if you are self-employed, is one of the following: "What's the going rate?" "What's a fair amount to charge?" "How much do I need to make?" "How much feels right for me to charge?" or even "How much can I tolerate charging without feeling guilty or having an anxiety attack?"

In our culture, men are often socialized to equate self-worth with success in work; women historically tend to rate themselves more according to success in intimate relationships. But as increasing numbers of women have entered the workforce in higher-level positions, they are becoming more and more susceptible to measuring their self-worth by the amount of money they make. So this equation of money with self-worth has become a serious problem for both sexes.

M Do you believe that Money = Self-worth?

If you think that you subscribe to this myth, ask yourself the following questions:
• Do you feel a lot better about yourself when you're making more money?
• Does the income of people close to you affect how much you respect them?
• Do you fear that people would look down on you if you underwent a salary cut, for any reason?
• Would being unemployed for a short period make you feel bad about yourself?
• Do you lose some respect for people if you find out that they are making much less money than you thought they were?

If you answered yes to three or more questions, then to some degree you believe that money equals self-worth. [To a small extent-Author.]

M Debunking Money = Self-worth

If you believe that your self-worth is tied to money, you need to look for examples that run counter to this powerful myth. Identify and describe, in as much detail as possible, a few people you know personally, or have read or heard about, who:
• Don't have a lot of money but, in your opinion, have an abundance of self-esteem. [Strong self image.]
• Have a lot of money but seem to have very little sense of self-worth. The next exercise for debunking this myth is as follows:
• Imagine something you could be doing with your life that wouldn't involve a lot of money but that would enhance your self-esteem or sense of self-worth.
• Write down a description of this activity or situation.

Bear in mind that for the time-being you're under no pressure to take action; just imagine this scenario. At some future time, you may want to take a concrete step towards your goal.

If you lose your job suddenly, it's in your best interest to discard the belief that money equals self-worth as quickly as possible. Tina's story will illustrate what I mean by this statement. Recently, she came to me for therapy after receiving notice that she was being laid off at work. Though she admitted that the job she held had been unsatisfying for the last two years, and that in her heart she knew it was time to move on, she was reeling from the shock of being laid off with two weeks' notice. She was doubting her abilities and feeling shaken in her self-esteem because her salary was removed abruptly and she was soon to be out of work. It took only a few sessions to help Tina disconnect her feelings of self-worth from this work trauma and start to reconnect with her real sense of energy and passion in work. Within a month, she was volunteering in a field she loved but had not had time to pursue. Within three months, she had been offered a position in that new, more creative arena. The beginning salary was slightly lower than that in her old job, but she felt no decrease in self-esteem. Quite the contrary: working in an area she loved increased her confidence and zest for life.

Since none of us had <u>perfect</u> parents, we go through life with <u>holes</u> in our psyches. We try to fill in the gaps through our jobs (as in Tina's case), our other achievements, our possessions, and, for some of us, by trying to make more and more money. But I believe the only way of truly enhancing our self-esteem and self-worth is to keep on working to fulfill more and more of our potential: to strive to be the best we can be in the areas of our life in which we feel passion and commitment. If we attach self-worth to the vagaries of the financial marketplace, we will be standing on shaky ground indeed. And the temporary admiration of others at our financial success can never ill us up over time in the same way that our own self-love and self-respect will.

MONEY = SECURITY

Money equals security is a very prevalent myth in our society, even though we tend to be a society of spenders rather than savers. Who among us does not believe, to a certain extent, that money is one of the main things that will provide us with some security' especially in our old age? [I do.] This money myth, like all the others, contains a kernel of truth. We do need enough financial security to make us feel at ease about our ability to take care of ourselves and our loved ones. But believing this money myth and investing too much emotional energy in it can be potentially destructive and even paralyzing.

Take David, for example. His uncle had gone bankrupt as a result of a bad business deal and had attempted suicide. This financial tragedy had such a profound effect on David's father that he worried all the time about not having enough money and lectured his children about the evils of frivolous spending. David grew up to be a lawyer who worked day and night to make money. He had an intense drive to have more and more money for his retirement years so he and his wife could live comfortably and still provide their three kids with a substantial inheritance. [Like me.] David was so worried about not having enough money that he never wanted to take even two weeks off at a time for vacations. He missed his daughter's sixth-grade concert and his son's eighth-grade play because he had to work both nights "to ensure his family's security," as he put it. He attacked his wife for buying a new living room couch when the old one was threadbare, calling this purchase an "unnecessary luxury." At the age of 48, he had the first of two heart attacks. With all this money, David was not secure. And if he died early, his <u>children</u>, the youngest of whom was six when the first heart attack struck, would not feel very secure and safe, even with more than enough money.

M Do you believe that Money = Security?
To see whether this money myth has a grip on you, ask yourself the following questions:
• When you think about not having a lot of money saved for the future, do you feel very uneasy and insecure?
• Do you judge people who spend a lot of money for present pleasures and short-term goals as being unwise and shortsighted?
• When you think about being secure in your old age, is having enough money the first thing (or the main thing) that comes to mind?

• Does putting money away in savings or in other "safe" investments give you a feeling of inner peace and security more than any other action does?
• If you have fears about your old age, does thinking about having more than enough money during that period comfort you and allay most of your fears?

If you answered yes to three or more of these questions, you probably believe that money equals security. [Yes I do to some extent-Author.]

M Debunking Money = Security

The tick in debunking this myth is to find a few examples that serve to contradict it. So I suggest that you identify and describe, in as much detail as possible, some elderly people you know who:
• Don't have a lot of money but seem very secure to you.
• Have a lot of money but don't seem at all secure.

What do you think is the difference between these people? What does one have that the other doesn't that leads to more real security?

Michael Phillips, author of The Seven Laws of Money and other good books, helped debunk this myth for me. He once said to me that when he looked around at the elderly people he knew and tied to determine who seemed truly secure, he found that money was not the determining factor. Of course, he acknowledged, elderly people do need enough money   for   the   basic necessities of life and for some pleasures and luxuries as well. But what distinguished these secure old people from the others was that they were not isolated; they were surrounded by a supportive network of friends of various ages. Goods and services were naturally exchanged in the course of their lives. Their friends were glad to take them grocery shopping or to shop for them; to accompany them to the movies or to invite them to dinner. So the prime ingredient in ensuing one's security in old age is social connectedness and lack of isolation, not   money.

Helen serves as an excellent example of what happens when an elderly person lives with wealth but in isolation. Although she resided in a luxurious retirement community in Florida, Helen disliked people and preferred to sit at home all day watching TV and smoking cigarettes. But sometimes she ruefully observed that because she had no fiends, she had to hire people to take her grocery shopping and to help her with other chores, and she would be completely on her own in a medical emergency. So even with all her money, Helen did not feel secure. When she was taken ill with a slow, debilitating form of cancer, she began to open up to people for the first time in years. She found loving help and support, and when she died, she was not alone and finally seemed at peace.

Granted, we do need [definitely] to save money for our retirement and/or our later years of life. But if we understand that money is not security, we'll lose some of our general anxiety about whether we're squirreling away enough of it. Instead, we'll be able to redirect some of this energy towards developing more satisfying and lasting personal contacts and friendships.

ASSESSING ALL THE MONEY MYTHS IN YOUR LIFE

You are now ready to take a collective look at all the money myths that have had an impact on your life. Consider:
• What are your most prevalent money myths?
• How have they been influencing your life?
• How have they affected your relationships - especially your love relationships?

• How would you like to modify these beliefs and the attitudes and behaviors that stem from them?
• What can you do, or what do you need to think about or tell yourself, to continue debunking the myths that prevent you from making rational decisions about your money?

Money does not equal 1) happiness, 2) love, 3) power, 4) freedom, 5) self-worth, or 6) security. Money equals dollars and cents, and is merely a tool to facilitate your attaining certain goals and having certain things. If you remember this, you won't be encumbered by anxiety, guilt, fear, or shame about how to earn, spend, save, or invest your money. Instead, you'll be able to use your money, both alone and in relationships, in a rational way that satisfies your real needs and wants, and that reflects your real values.

"Money Harmony: Resolving Money conflicts in Your Life and Relationships" by Olivia Mellan. It shows you how your hidden, intense thoughts and feelings about money may be preventing you from dealing with it effectively and causing major stress in your life and relationships. [I highly recommend this book to your readers-Author.]

A Money Story

Take out a one dollar bill and look at it. The one dollar bill you're looking at first came off the presses in 1957 in its present design. This so-called paper money is in fact a cotton and linen blend, with red and blue minute silk fibers running through it. It is actually material. We've all washed it without it falling apart. A special blend of ink is used, the contents we will never know. (Big Treasury Department secret). It is overprinted with symbols and then it is starched to make it water resistant and pressed to give it that nice crisp look. If you look on the front of the bill, you will see the United States Treasury Seal. On the top you will see the scales for the balance-a balanced budget. In the center you have a carpenter's T-square, a tool used for an even cut. Underneath is the key to the United States Treasury. That's all pretty easy to figure out, but what is on the back of that dollar bill is something we should all know.

If you turn the bill over, you will see two circles. Both circles, together comprise the Great Seal of the United States. The First Continental Congress requested that Benjamin Franklin and a group of men come up with a Seal. It took them four years to accomplish this task and another two years to get it approved. If you look at the left hand circle, you will see a Pyramid. Notice the face is lighted and the western side is dark. This country was just beginning. We had not begun to explore the West or decided what we could do for Western Civilization. The Pyramid is un-capped, again signifying that we were not even close to being   finished.   Inside   the capstone you have the all-seeing eye, and ancient symbol for divinity. It was Franklin's belief that one man couldn't do it alone, but a group of men, with the help of God, could do anything. "IN GOD WE TRUST" is on this currency. The means "God has favored our undertaking." The Latin below the pyramid, NOVUS ORDO SECLORUM, means "a new order has begun." At the base of the pyramid is the Roman Numeral for 1776.

If you look at the right-hand circle, and check it carefully, you will learn that it is on every National Cemetery in the United States. It is also on the Parade of Flags Walkway at   the

Bushnell, Florida National Cemetery and is the centerpiece of most hero's monuments. Slightly modified, it is the seal of the President of the United States and it is always visible whenever he speaks, yet no one knows what the symbols mean. The Bald Eagle was selected as a symbol for victory for two reasons: first, he is not afraid of a storm; he is strong and he is smart enough to soar above it. Secondly, he wears no material crown. We had just broken from the King of England. Also, notice the shield is unsupported. This country can now stand on its own. At the top of that shield you have a white bar signifying congress, a unifying factor. We were coming together as one nation. In the Eagle's beak you will read, "E PLURTBUS UNUM." meaning "one nation from many people." Above the Eagle you have thirteen stars representing the thirteen original colonies, and any clouds of misunderstanding rolling away. Again, we were coming together as one. Notice what the Eagle holds in his talons. He holds an olive branch and arrows. This country wants peace, but we will never be afraid to fight to preserve peace. The Eagle always wants to face the olive branch, but in time of war, his gaze turns toward the arrows.

Lucky Number Thirteen (13):
They say that the number 13 is an unlucky number. This is almost a worldwide belief. You will usually never see a room numbered 13, or any hotels or motels with a 13th floor. But, think about this: 13 original colonies, 13 signers of the Declaration of Independence, 13 stripes on our lag, 13 steps on the Pyramid, 13 letters in the Latin above, 13 letter in "E Pluribus Unum,"
13 star's above the Eagle, 13 plumes of feathers on each span of the Eagle's wing, 13 bars on that shield, 13 leaves on the olive branch, 13 fruits, and if you look closely, 13 arrows. Tell everyone what is on the back of the one dollar bill and what is stands for, because nobody else will.

CHAPTER VII

CHAPTER   VII
Financial Security

Here are five (5) very important questions concerning this chapter:

1) <u>What</u> is financial security?

2) <u>How</u> can you get it?

3) <u>Who</u> can help you get it?

4) <u>How</u> can you learn more about it?

5) Can you <u>lose</u> it?

1) What is Financial Security?
(It's two words:)

<u>Financial</u> = Relating to money (Finance) and its use and distribution:

[i.e., Finance = a) Money or other liquid resources of a Government; business; group; or Individual; b) the system that includes the circulation of money; the granting of credit; the making of investments; and the provision of banking facilities; c) the science or study of the management of funds; d) the obtaining of funds or capital.]

<u>Security</u> = The quality or state of being secure as a) freedom from danger, b) freedom from FEAR or anxiety, c) freedom from want or deprivation.

I believe Financial Security, therefore, is having enough money (and/or other assets, etc.) to provide funds to purchase your needs (and a <u>few</u> wants): And a mental 'state of mind' in which you are free from constant worry about having the bare necessities of life. Also, to live with a little dignity, a feeling of not being a burden to someone else, and a decent self image (self-esteem).

Security Blanket
A blanket carried by a child as a protection against anxiety; or, a saving account, or accounts, held by adults (Christian and secular) whose existence dispels anxiety concerning the future.

Almost everyone in the world wants financial security. Unfortunately, unless you live in the United States or one of a few other democratic countries, your chances of obtaining it are somewhere between slim and none! Even if you live in the U.S., it is still very possible that you do not have financial security. I am very sorry to report this sad fact of 21st century.   Most
Christians want financial security also, it's natural. Even though they have complete and total

security when they get to Heaven, they (at least I) still do not enjoy going without and/or being dependent upon fiends and/or relatives, or their church.

2) How can you get it (Financial Security)?

It is really very simple. Work hard and then work harder yet. SAVE. Study and go to school, and most important of all Pray daily that God will provide financial security for you and your family. God does not necessarily want all Christians to be poor. Most Christians with money are very generous to others less fortunate than themselves and give lots of money to the work of Christ (Church, Missionaries, etc.).

Making INVESTMENTS is the generally accepted way to provide future financial security for yourself and family. The best investment anyone can make is to purchase a home (and/or real estate). Also, but not necessarily in order a few are listed herewith: a) stocks/bonds (individual);
b) mutual funds (groups of stocks and bonds); c) silver, gold, platinum and precious metals; d) valuable stones (diamonds, rubies, emeralds, etc.); e) oil paintings; f) rental (investments) real estate; g) retirement accounts (401K, 403B, etc.); h) I.R.A.'s (of various types); I) antiques; j) classic cars - trucks; k) church bonds; 1) etc., etc., etc.

However, if you do not want to take any unnecessary risks (except of course that of inflation) with your servings, just keep them in bank savings and/or money market accounts.   U.S.
Government insured securities such as Treasury Bills, T-Notes, T-Bonds, and other issues are also risk-fee. Even though your interest income will be relatively low you cannot lose your life savings and you probably will sleep much better at night. I believe that if you are somewhat of a anxious or conservative person, being safe is better than the possibility of being sorry.

If you will look at an compound interest savings chart, (you can obtain them from your bank) or (stationary store), you will see that if you even save a 'little' money every month (I realize that is not easy for most people) you will have a very decent amount of cash to assist you with your retirement. There are several good books about investments and how to   get   financial security. The Bible, of course, is your Best resource as usual. Finally, in Mark 10:29, Jesus tells us that... "no one who has left his home or family, for me and the gospel, will fail to receive a 100 times as much in this present age... (with persecutions) and in the age to come,   eternal life."

3L Who can help you get it (Financial Security)?

God is the best Financial Adviser that you can have. He has your best interests at heart and he will never steal from you (unlike a lot of other advisers you might select). Also, He will never give you 'Bad' financial advice because He is the only one who 'knows' the future. In addition to God, I strongly recommend that you obtain the services of an: a) C.F.P. Citified Financial Planner (a retirement expect); b) C.P.A. (Citified Public Accountant);   c)   Banker   (Vice President); and last but not least; d) Attorney (sooner or later you are going to need one, trust me on this). In today's 'litigious' society, it is a necessity of life. Ninety percent (90%) of all of the Lawyers in the world live in the United States!

Always remember it is <u>yours</u> (and Gods) money ($) not your advisor's. Obtain the best advise you can from the expects (and those listed above), then you make the final investment decisions based upon their opinions and much prayer.

In investing to obtain your financial security for the future, please keep in mind that in most cases you are taking some risk (Risk versus Return). If you take a lot of risk you, you
conceivably may get a much higher return. You, however, also conversely could lose your Life Savings!

I strongly recommend that you make investments with <u>little</u>, or no, risk. I really do. Yes I know all about inflation, etc., however, If you lose your savings, you just may never be able to get them back again. [I was not able to-Author.]

Look at all of the millions and millions of people who have lost all, or most, of their life savings in the stock market during the past 2 years. Also, inflation has ran at about only two percent (2%) for the past 10 years! Remember the old saying (I just love old sayings, don't you?) "If it sounds too good to be true, it probably is." If you have a successful friend, or relative who is very trustworthy, they would be another source of advice on how to get your financial security. Another good idea is to ask someone at your local church, if you know   a   church member, etc., who is financially secure, knowledgeable, honest, and will keep your information confidential.

<u>4) How can you learn more about it (Financial Security)?</u>

Take time to read several books on this very important subject. There are many, many of them out there. Also, read and study your Bible. There is a lot more information in it about money then you would believe. Ask questions of the 'experts.' Ask them a lot of questions: and, then <u>pray</u> for financial knowledge, and especially for financial <u>wisdom</u>.

I realize that most of your readers out there, are very, very busy most all of the time. You must, however, make time to do some much needed research, and study, so that you do not lose your financial security just because you were too busy to properly research your investments. I pray that you properly research your investments. I hope that you know your brokers (etc.) will get their commissions whether you make money or lose money on your transactions. Be very careful with your life savings (financial security). That is why they call them life savings, "It takes your <u>whole</u> hard working life to save them up." [Author.]

As with "who can help you get financial security?" (see number 3 above) some good sources to <u>lean</u> (glean) from are: a) C.F.P., b) C.P.A., c) bankers, d) lawyers, e) experts, f) Bible,   g) financial successful friends or relatives, h) pastors, and, I) wise church members or staff.

<u>Please allow me to ask this question?</u> Can you lean to play: tennis, golf, baseball, football, soccer, basketball, softball, chess, cards, or cook, sew, decorate, etc? <u>Without</u> spending a lot of time practicing, and reading? Likewise, leaning about financial security requires a 'lot' of time spent in reading, researching, and practicing and praying.

I believe that the more you learn about your financial security, the better your chances are of obtaining it. Period!

5) Can you loose it (Financial Security)?

Oh yes, real, real easy. All you have to do is BLINK, once! Really, I am not kidding. I should know, I did and I am somewhat of an expert on Money. As you can see if you have read any of my four (4) books or know anything about my 35 years banking and business background. I do not really understand the economics of it, however, losing financial security seems to be one of the easiest things in the world to do. Just a few ways (and there are many) to lose it are: a) serious illness, b) loss of job, c) divorce, d) stock market crash, e) real estate market crash, f) recession, g) depression, h) desolation of non cash/R.E. assets and; I) taking care of children and/or parents in desperate need; j) etc., etc., etc. My friend, because it is so, so very easy to lose your financial security: "Make sure to lay up some of your treasure in Heaven (where no thieves, jokers on your right or clowns on your left, can steal from you or rob you." As I have stated, you certainly and to easily, can lose your 'earthly' financial security. You cannot, however, ever lose your blessed hope of 'Heavenly' financial security. Trust me, and the Bible, on that important spiritual fact.

Note:
If you should lose your life savings, and I personally pray that you do not, please remember that God is faithful (even if we sometimes are not). He will take care of your financial security. He said I will never leave you nor forsake you. That, my dear reader, includes providing you with your basic human needs and essential security. I have read that many wealthy (secure) people, have lost all of their savings, at least once during their lives. Some of them have even lost all of their money ($) 2 or 3 times. Therefore, if you should lose your savings, daily pray that God
will restore them to you (at least enough for all of your basic needs) like he did for Job in the Bible. [One of my Favorite books-Author.]

Seven simple repairs for your 401K. 403B. etc.

For the nation's estimated 40 million 401 (k) investors, the past two years have been a shocking reversal of fortune. After nearly a decade (10 years) of double-digit returns. Now many 401 (k) investors are facing major losses in their portfolios, often for the first time ever. So what do you do when your 401(k) turns into a 201(k)? (50% as much as before):

Let's get one thing clear: No one is suggesting that investors react to every market gyration by frantically shifting money around. But the fact is, the majority of 401(k) participants lack a clear retirement investment strategy, and their portfolios are overdue for an overhaul.

A study by benefits firm Hewit Associates found that 36 percent of 401(k) participants invest in only one fund and another 19 percent in just two funds, which suggests that workers are badly under-diversified. And nearly 60 percent don't save enough to get their employer's full match, leaving free money on the table. So isn't it time to stat improving your portfolio's performance? Yes, it clearly is. Here's a seven-step 401(k) ix-up:

1. Figure Out Where You Stand

If you haven't opened your 401(k) statement lately, grit your teeth and do it. Make a list of all your retirement portfolios-a spouse's 401(k), a rollover IRA, and so on-and add up how much you have in each fund (software such as Quicken or Microsoft Money can help you immensely).

Next, determine what kinds of stocks your funds contain-large-cap growth, mid-cap value, etc. If you want to go a step further, look beyond the fund's sector and find out what stocks the manager actually buys. Legg Mason Value Trust fund, for example, has been peppered with growth companies like Amazon.com and Dell, while roughly a third of the stocks in Fidelity's Equity Income n fund don't pay dividends. Check a fund's holdings by looking at its annual report online; you can also get a portfolio analysis on sites such as Momingstar.com.

Don't be surprised if you're more heavily weighted in risky stocks than you realized. Take a couple we know. Two years ago, he, a 38-year-old corporate executive in Minneapolis, Minn., rolled over a 401(k) from his old job into a new account with a broker and invested almost the entire amount in tech stocks. As of early April, that account had dropped 87 percent from its $63,000 peak in March 2000. (Sad but true.)

Luckily, the rest of their retirement money was less tech-heavy; all told, their combined portfolios, now totaling $249,000, are down by only 29 percent.

2. Get Serious About Saving

One sure way to make up for lost ground is to put more money aside. In fact, it's quite possible that, emboldened by the stock market's supersize returns, you weren't saving enough in the first place. Now it's time to reassess. Online calculators (available on inancialengines.com or Morningstar's Clear Future) can help you estimate what you'll need to save. Count on an annual growth rate of seven percent for a divers led portfolio.

Watch Your Assets

These sample portfolios reflect a simple truth: Not every person stats withdrawing from a 401(k) on his or her 65th birthday. So the asset mixes below, devised by Scot Lummer of the online investment firm mPower, are pegged to the retirement date of your choice.

A. Long-Term Plan. In the early stages of your career, keep almost all of your 401(k) in stock funds. Gradually add bonds in your forties and fifties. Even if you're uneasy with the risk of the stock market, stash at least 55% in equities.

B. Five Years to Retirement. It's time to get serious about protecting your kitty [your Financial Security-Author]. Stocks should comprise no . more than 60% of your overall portfolio; if you have significant nonretirement assets, you can keep up to 80% of 401 (k) balances in equities.

C. In Retirement. Ideally, you will live a long time-which means you need to keep some money, about 35%, in stocks. If your net

worth and risk tolerance are both high, you can stake as much as 55% in stocks.

Once you work through the numbers, you will be shocked by how much you need to sock away to finance your retirement. [Trust me on this-Author.] The Vanguard Group, for instance,

calculates that the average investor earning $100,000 will need to stash about 20 percent of his or her salary, including a company match, over 30 years to retire by age 67 with a $75,000

annual income, (and That assumes full Social Security benefits.)

The good news: Your 401 (k) plan can help you achieve your savings goal with its instant tax savings on contributions, tax-deferred growth and, (for most workers), company matches. So contribute the most [maximum] allowable. Saving six percent now? Try pumping that to ten percent. [Someday you will be glad you did-Author.]

3. Scramble Your Nest Egg

The recent market drop [and its continued volatility] is a reminder that diversification is essential to protect against wipeouts. So review your overall split between stocks and bonds-this proportion will have the biggest impact on your retunes and your risk level. Anyone over 30 should consider adding a small dose of bonds to the 401 (k) for ballast.

Next, divvy up your equity allocation more finely between funds that hold large stocks, small stocks and international equities, and between growth funds and value funds.

Remember: Your 401(k) remains the rudder guiding your entire portfolio. "With a 401(k), you can make tax-free, low cost adjustments," points out Dimensional Fund Advisors. "In a taxable account, you may be hard-pressed to make changes because of taxes and trading costs."

4. Beware Company: Stock Time Bombs

About 20 percent of workers have a 401 (k) that offers company stock. If yours is one of them, consider this cautionary tale from Michael, president of a Group, an Annapolis, Md., 401(k) ad¬ vice firm. He recently got a call from a 58-year-old Lucent employee. Early last year the man had $400,000 in his 401(k), 90 percent in Lucent stock, and he planned to retire in two years. Then Lucent's stock tumbled; his account is now worth only $40,000.   [Tragic?-is   it   not-Author.]

We can't say it enough: Don't put more than ten percent of your 401 (k) into any <u>single</u> equity, especially company stock. "You are taking a tremendous amount of risk for average returns," says an UCLA accounting professor.

If you are required to own employer shares as a matching contribution, there are ways to offset your risk. Choose stock funds that invest in industries that do not move in sync with your own company.

5. Make Your Move

Now you're ready to bring your portfolio in line with your ideal allocation. The question is: Do you move your money all at once or in gradual adjustments?

Most participants make changes by redirecting new money, but this method takes too long. Instead, advisers recommend moving existing 401 (k) assets to make an immediate change. Another strategy, suggests and financial adviser of Chatham, N.J., is to move a potion of your money every month for six months until your allocations are realigned. That way, if a particular sector recovers, you'll capture gains.

6. Rebalance. Rebalance and Rebalance Again

Over time, market moves will throw your portfolio out of whack, so you'll need to rebalance. This keeps your allocations on target, dramatically cuts risk, and may add another half a percent yearly to your return over the long term. Why? Because when you rebalance, you typically sell better performers and buy out-of-favor laggards. While that's difficult psychologically, it's a key to success: You sell high and buy low.

B, O and S, an investment advisory firm, compared results for two portfolios, each worth $100,000 as of January 1, 1998, and allocated identically: 25 percent in the Vanguard Total Bond Market index, 25 percent in the Janus Fund, 25 percent in the Dodge & Cox Stock Fund, and 25 percent in the Artisan International Fund. New contributions—$10,000 a year to each account—followed the same allocation. As of this March 31, portfolio No. 1—rebalanced at the end of each year-was worth $189,760. The untouched portfolio? Only $183,884.

Check allocations every 12 months at least. "You're teaching yourself to be a contrarian," says an investment adviser ofelicientfrontier.com. "You're selling when everyone else is euphoric, which takes guts."

7. Call in the Pros

As your 401(k) grows and your finances become more complicated, you may [you will-Author] need to consult an expert, especially if you're nearing retirement. Many 401 (k) plans   offer advice, whether online or in person. If your plan doesn't meet your needs, search for financial planners at websites like fpanet.org or napfa.org, and ask friends for recommendations.

After renovating your 401 (k), you'll be on your way to a more secure [Financial Secuity Author] retirement,

CHAPTER VIII

CHAPTER VIII
The Federal Reserve System

The Nation's Money Manager

Unlike other major Nations where strong central banks were the rule, the United States throughout the 19th century relied on a patchwork banking system that in effect left the nation's economic welfare to chance. And the nation paid the price of that errant policy.

Not that there were no precedents for a central bank in our history. There were two abortive attempts to create a lasting central banking system. Alexander Hamilton was the founding spirit of the First Bank of the United States which survived from 1791 until 1811. In 1816, the
Second Bank of the United States was established. It too was allowed to lapse in 1836. Its demise was followed by the "Panic of 1837." Panic describes the situation well. For until the Federal Reserve System was established, the nation fell victim to a series of severe economic dislocations known as "money panics."

The underlying reasons for panics were many and complex, but the results were obvious. There was not enough money to go around. Typically, banks were pressed by heavy demands   for
currency. Since the supply of money was inelastic, institutions that had to have cash called in loans from their customers creating a "panic psychology." Depositors reacted as was to be
expected by withdrawing funds and in the process created additional stress for the banks. All of this had a ippling effect that led to widespread panics and failures of many banks that were basically quite sound. There were other problems too. A bewildering array of notes issued by banks as money; the fluctuating value of bank notes; epidemics of counterfeiting; and the lack of central supervision over the banking system.

After still another economic crisis - the "Panic of 1907" - the nation had had enough. Congress responded in 1908 by forming a National Monetary Commission whose recommendations led to legislation known as the Federal Reserve Act. Signed into law by President Woodrow Wilson on December 23, 1913, the act was designed "to provide for the   establishment   of   Federal
Reserve Banks, to furnish an elastic currency, to afford means of rediscounting commercial
paper, to establish a more effective supervision of banking in the United States, and for other purposes." Ultimately, then, panic had led to order and the creation of an agency serving as the central bank of the United States. The agency has since unofficially come to be known as "the Fed." Its responsibility in brief is to act as the "nation's money manager."

The Structure of the Federal Reserve System

THE BOARD OF GOVERNORS

The Fed is a unique blend of public and private interests that promotes the national welfare. At the heart of the Federal Reserve System, is the Board of Governors in Washington, D.C. The

139

Board is composed of 7 members appointed by the President and confirmed by the Senate. Appointments are for 14 years, with one term expiring every two years. These long terms, were mandated by Congress to remove the Board of Governors from political pressure and enable the governors to act independently and in the best interests of all the people. For this reason the Federal Reserve System is termed a quasi-governmental or independent government agency.

The Board determines general operating policies for the System as a whole and formulates the rules and regulations necessary to carry out the purposes of the Federal Reserve   Act.   Its principal duties consist of exerting an influence over credit conditions and supervising the Federal Reserve Banks and member banks.

THE FEDERAL RESERVE BANKS

To insure that the Federal Reserve System would be attuned to the unique needs and differences apparent in a nation that spanned 3000 miles and linked together fishing villages   in   New England and Indian reservations in the West, Congress instituted a regional system of banks. On the same day - November 16 - in 1914, the 12 Federal Reserve Banks were opened   for business. The banks with their branches are as follows:

District	Federal Reserve Bank of	Branches
1	Boston	None
2	New York	Buffalo, N. Y.
3	Philadelphia	None
4	Cleveland	Cincinnati, Ohio
		Pittsburgh, Pa.
	Richmond	Baltimore, Md.
		Charlotte, N.C.
	Atlanta	Birmingham, Ala.
		Jacksonville, Fla.
		Nashville, Tenn.
		New Orleans, La.
7	Chicago	Detroit, Mich.
8	St. Louis	Little Rock, Ark.
		Louisville, Ky.
		Memphis, Tenn.
9	Minneapolis	Helena, Mont.
10	Kansas City	Denver, Colo.
		Oklahoma City,
		Okla. Omaha, Neb.
11	Dallas	El Paso, Tex.
		Houston, Tex.
		San Antonio, Tex.
12	San Francisco	Los Angeles, Ca.

FEDERAL ADVISORY COUNCIL

Acting in an advisory capacity, this council confers with the Board of Governors on general business conditions and makes recommendations concerning matters within the jurisdiction of the Federal Reserve System. The 12-member council is made up of 1 member from each of the Federal Reserve districts. Each member is drawn from the commercial banking community and is appointed for a term of one year. The Federal Advisory Council meets in Washington at least four times annually, and more often if called into special session by the Board of Governors.

MEMBER BANKS

Directly and indirectly the Fed serves all of the nation's 14,000 commercial banks. Of this total, about 5,700 or roughly 40 per cent belong to the Federal Reserve System. Fed members,
however, account for about 78 per cent of the total deposits held by the nation's banks. Moreover, they have nearly 18,000 offices, branches and other facilities or over 60 per cent of all commercial banking offices in the United States.

Who belongs to the system? By law all national banks are required to be members. State chartered banks that qualify may be admitted to membership.

What the Fed Does

What exactly does a central bank do?

It functions as the nation's "money manager" by providing such essential services as these:
• Supplying coin and currency. Federal Reserve notes make up about 99 per cent of the paper money in general circulation in the U.S. There is about $70 billion in coin and currency
now in circulation. When a bank needs money, it orders it from the Fed. In addition, the Fed removes won or damaged coin and currency from circulation.
• Check processing. System-wide the Fed processes 10 billion checks annually representing about $5 trillion.
• Fiscal agent of the United States government. The Fed maintains the largest checking account in the world - that of the United States government. All checks drawn on the Treasury are ultimately paid at Federal Reserve Bank!>.
• Marketing of government securities. When the U.S. Treasury needs to borrow money to pay for the government's operations, the Fed sells government securities such as Treasury bills, bonds and notes. It services government securities by issuing, replacing and redeeming
them.
• Control of credit. The Fed sets margin requirements for purchasing securities to prevent the misuse of credit. With other agencies, it shares in enforcing truth in lending laws designed to protect consumers by assuring that the cost of financing is clearly stated.

• Loans. Member banks have the option of borrowing funds from the Fed.

Monetary Policy—the Fed's Number One Job

The Fed is charged with carrying out all the duties above - and others. But the responsibility of determining monetary policy is its most vital service to the nation.

Basically, monetary policy is determining the right supply of money and credit the nation needs to stay economically healthy. If there is too little money and credit, the economy may slow
down and fall into a recession. Too much, on the other hand, and there is danger that the economy may overheat and suffer from serious inflation.

FOMC

The Fed deals with monetary policy through its Federal Open Market Committee [FOMC] which consists of the seven members of the Board of Governors and the Presidents of five Reserve Banks. The president of the Federal Reserve Bank of New York is a permanent member of FOMC, while the other four presidents are selected on a rotating basis. All 12 presidents, however, attend the sessions of FOMC.

Each month FOMC sets the guidelines for the volume of money and credit to serve the United States. The committee's monetary policy decisions are based on the economic intelligence
reports assembled by the Board and the 12 Federal Reserve Banks. Monetary policy is designed to achieve full employment, economic growth, stable prices and a satisfactory balance   of
payments.

RESERVES. DISCOUNT RATE. OPEN MARKET

How does FOMC affect the money supply?

Its primary tools are (1) bank reserves, (2) the discount rate and (3) open market operations.

Each member bank is required by law to set aside a certain per cent of its customers' deposits as reserves. These banks must keep reserves at the district Federal Reserve Bank or as cash in their own vaults. By increasing or decreasing the level of reserves in the banking system, the Federal Reserve makes it harder or easier for banks to make loans or buy securities. So, for instance, if the Fed lowers reserve requirements, it frees up additional funds in the banking system that can be used to make additional loans. And vice versa.

The discount rate is the interest rate member banks pay when they borrow from reserve banks. A higher discount rate tends to discourage borrowing and therefore has a tendency to restrict economic activity. A lower rate makes it more attractive to borrow.

Of all the tools that the Fed has to influence economic activity, it most frequently relies on open market operations. To lower bank reserves (and therefore tighten the money supply), the Fed sells government securities. Since buyers pay for securities by giving the Fed checks drawn on commercial banks, the immediate result is to draw down on the bank reserves and restrict lending activity. To do the opposite, the Fed buys government securities and issues its checks to sellers who deposit them in commercial banks and thereby increase reserves in the banking system. The banks then have more funds available for lending and the money supply is expanded.

Who Pays the Cost of Running the Fed?

Federal Reserve Banks generate their own income from two main sources.

• The first (and major) source is interest from government securities, which are purchased and held by the Reserve System to influence the volume of bank reserves in the nation. Last year the Fed earned about $5 billion from its government portfolio.

• The second source of income is interest charged on loans granted to member banks. This earned the Fed about $15 million last year.

Any earnings in excess of expenses are transferred to the U.S. Treasury. Generally the cost of running the Fed has required about 9% per cent of its earnings, dividends to member banks have totaled about 1 % per cent and the remaining 90% per cent has been paid back to the Treasury. Last year from its earnings the Fed paid the Treasury over $4.3 billion.

The Federal Reserve Bank of San Francisco and its 2,200 employees at head office and its branches in Los Angeles, Portland, Salt Lake City and Seattle stand ready to serve you. If you live in Alaska, Arizona (except for the southeastern comer), California, Guam, Hawaii, Idaho, Nevada, Oregon, Utah or Washington, you're in the 12th Distinct territory of the Federal Reserve Bank of San Francisco.

U.S. Federal Statement of revenues and Expenses

Revenues

	Fiscal Year' 2001	2002	Change from 2001
Individual income taxes	$944,339,000,000	858,344,000,000	-14%
Social insurance taxes2	693,967,000,000	700,762,000,000	1%
User fees, earmarked taxes and receipts3.	415,036,000,000	430,247,000,000,	4%
Corporation taxes	151,075,000,000	148,042,000,000	-2%
Excise taxes and customs duties	85,600,000,000	85,591,000,000	0%
Miscellaneous receipts	37,664,000,000	34,040,000,000	-10%
Death taxes4	28,400,000,000	26,507,000,000	-7%
Total Revenues	$2,406,081,000,000	2,283,533,000,000	■5%

Expenses

Social spending5	$1,287,666,000,000	1,398,221,000,000	9%
Interest on national debt	359,508,000,000	332,537,000,000	-8%
Military spending	287,998,000,000	309,527,000,000	7%
Administrative agencies6	199,762,000,000	205,057,000,000	3%
Transportation ,	57,177,000,000	61,780,000,000	
Post-9/11 emergency funding7	2,475,000,000	44,212,000,000	
State and foreign affairs8	31,794,000,000	34,767,000,000	9%
Environment, fish, wildlife, parks and interior9	30,287,000,000	32,100,000,000	6%
NASA	14,094,000,000	14,321,000,000	2%
Judiciary	4,795,000,000	5,281,000,000	10%
Congress	2,024,000,000	2,054,000,000	1%
The President	1,224,000,000	1,326,000,000	8%
Total Expenses	$2,278,804,000,000	2,441,183,000,000	7%
Surplus/(Deficit)"	$127,277,000,000	(157,650,000,000)	

Notes

1. The U.S. Government fiscal year begins on October 1 and ends on September 30.
2. Includes direct taxes and payroll taxes from individuals and employers for disability insurance, Social Security and other federal retirement programs, hospital insurance taxes, and unemployment insurance taxes.
3. Represents receipts of federal departments and agencies netted from gross outlays in Treasury reports, such as proprietary receipts from the public, receipts from off-budget federal entities, and total undistributed offsetting receipts.
4. Repealed effective January 1, 2010, by Public Law 107-16 signed by President Bush on June 7, 2001.
5. Includes arts, education, labor, health and human services, low income and public housing, WIC, welfare block grants, food stamps and other agricultural programs, and federal retirement programs (including Social Security).
6. Includes SBA, GSA, DOE, GAO, Commerce, CPB, Distinct of Columbia, EEOC, Export-Import Bank, FCC, FDIC, FEMA, FTC, Government Printing Office, Justice, Library of Congress, National Archives and independent agencies.
7. Reflects outlays for anti-terrorism initiatives, disaster relief, bioterrorism response, border security, intergovernmental joint investigation and prosecution, and air transportation security.
8. Includes outlays for Department of State, Peace Corps, OPIC, AID, foreign military sales, and other international assistance programs.
9. Includes EPA, National Park Service, Fish and Wildlife Service, Bureau of Land Management, Forest Service, National Oceanic and Atmospheric Administration, and major environmental programs of federal agencies.
10. The excess of Social Security taxes over outlays for Social Security was $163 billion in 2001 and $159 billion in 2002. Exclusion of Social Security taxes and benefit payments from revenues and expenses would result in a deficit of $33 billion in 2001 and a deficit of $316 billion in 2002.

CONCLUSION

Lest the reader of this "For the Love of Money" (Part I) think that I am presenting a biased picture of the said author (me, ha, ha), let me point out at this moment in time that that assumption would be totally and completely incorrect. I will be the first to admit that I am just a sinner saved by God's grace. I am not perfect (sinless); have never in my life been perfect and, more Importantly, I will not be perfect in the future either. Once I get to Heaven, however, I promise you a whole new and improved me. I read in the Bible about great men of God sinning (doing something wrong). I have read many, many books and articles of famous Christian people who ready admit their mistakes . Billy Graham, Franklin Graham, etc. It really makes me nervous when I am around Christians who say they never do anything wrong. I refer to those Christians as: Pious, Self-Righteous, Sanctimonious, Hypocrites! Some act like they never sin any longer? I am not one of those types. I never have been, and never could be. One last time NOW, I am a sinner, I have always been a sinner, and I always will be a sinner until I get to heaven. I pray that will be very soon now. (Absent from the body = Present with the Lord.) Some people will undoubtedly tell you that I am not perfect, and that I have made many, many mistakes in my life. I want you to know that I agree with them. The only little problem I would have with most of those people is that they seem to feel that they have never done anything wrong? Let us pray for their enlightenment.

AFTERWARD

Alan was very definitely was a confirmed Fundamental Christian Believer. As he was the First to admit, however, NOT a great Nor even a good Christian. Yet, he Was very much a dedicated life-long Christian. There is absolutely 'no' doubt about this very important spiritual fact. That is, in the mind of any true believers, Period.

Yes, he lost his way (sinned) many, many times during his hard, sad, and tumultuous life [filled with SO many 'Trials and Tabulations'] here on 'old' planet earth. He NEVER, however, ever lost his Faith in his Beloved Lord and Savior [Jesus Christ]. Nor, did he EVER Deny the Lord, even when he was right at deaths front door, several times. No, not once.

Alan suffered a Horrendous amount of very difficult situations and circumstances; Severe Emotional Hurt; Major Physical Pain; Not to even mention the Betrayal by his first wife;

closest love ones; 'so called' fiends; his family; sons and church members. The church is the only army in the world that shoots its hurt and wounded. I do not understand that at all? They shot Him!

He knew who he was, an old banker-sinner saved by God's redeeming Grace and the Blood of His son, Jesus. You did not need to remind him of that fact, although several not so nice people did exactly that. Alan knew his Only strength [just one] and he also knew very well, his many, many weaknesses [even better than all of his mortal arch-enemies].

Alan knew very well who His Maker was [God] and had made Peace with him Long ago. Here is a man who truly loved Others much more than himself. He dedicated his entire adult life to Helping the poor, needy and less fortunate souls. Also, missionaries; pastors; friends; co-workers; church members and young people; just to mention a few.

Whenever, God calls him home to a 'better' place (Heaven) he wishes those who would mourn his Home going (if any, ha-ha) not to be sad but to be happy. He just never fit in down here on earth. He will, when he gets to his 'real' home with his Heavenly Father. Also, then he will be re-united with his beloved mother whom he misses so, so very much. I John 1:9, Book of Job, Romans 10:9 & John 3:16.

To any more knowledgeable and wiser critic's out there who feel that this book may be either: incomplete; incorrect; and/or uninformative on the volumes topic of money; I totally agree with you and God bless you anyway!

www.ingramcontent.com/pod-product-compliance
Lightning Source LLC
Chambersburg PA
CBHW060920040426
42445CB00011B/714